DATE			

FORM 125 M

EXOTIC VEGETABLES

OTHER KRAFT BOOKS

The Best of American Gardening
Grow Your Own Dwarf Fruit Trees
Growing Food the Natural Way
The Home Garden Cookbook
Fruits for the Home Garden
Luther Burbank, the Wizard and the Man
Rainbow by the Bayou
Gardener, Go Home
Garden to Order
Give Father a Hard Knock
The Birds and the Beasts Were There
Land of Milk and Omelets

EXOTIC VEGETABLES

HOW TO GROW AND COOK THEM

By KEN and PAT KRAFT

WALKER AND COMPANY
New York

This book is for Dr. Vernon F. Lightfoot, with gratitude and affection.

CONTENTS

ACKNOWLEDGMENTS

As with any book of this nature, the friendly help and the expert knowledge of many persons—seedsmen, plant breeders, gardeners, librarians, horticulturists, and more—have been of immense help. We are most grateful to all of them, and although space precludes a more complete acknowledgment, we take this opportunity to thank, specifically: Miss Kate Alfriend, U.S. Department of Agriculture, Office of Communication; Jonathan Burpee, Gerald F. Burke, Miss Jeannette Lowe, and Ted Torrey of W. Atlee Burpee Company; Fred Cramer of T. Sakata & Company; J. A. Demonchaux of J. A. Demonchaux Company; Miss Barbara Lowenstein; Miss Christine Oram of Thompson & Morgan; the staff of the Santa Rosa-Sonoma County Public Library; Richard Tracy of the *Sacramento Bee*; David Tsang and Denis Ma of Tsang & Ma International; and Charles B. Wilson of Joseph Harris Company.

WELCOME TO ADVENTURE

We are inviting you to come along on an adventure—in fact, on two adventures. One is in the garden: an enchantment of growing a whole panoply of vegetables appreciated abroad but rarely, if ever, found in American gardens today. The other? An adventure in taste: cooking and savoring these exotics, starting with the delicious little morsel called adzuki bean, and on through the crisp cee gwa, buttery orach, tart sorrel, and at last the mild and handsome Welsh onion.

All told, there are sixty-one plants and about 250 kitchen tips and recipes for them. We felt there would be no point in explaining how to grow a plant many American gardeners had never heard of, let alone seen, unless we could also tell what it tastes like and how to prepare it for the table. In selecting which vegetables to include, we put the most weight on their probable taste appeal to Americans. The second criterion was each plant's willingness to grow in this country, given the right conditions. Third, we included only those plants for which you can get seed, be they cardoon, scorzonera, Hinn Choy, or fraises des bois. We have named the houses that carry the seeds in each case and have listed them with addresses at the end of the book.

Wherever we have included a plant that will be familiar to some of the gardeners who may read this book, we did so because most gardeners don't know or grow this vegetable. That has, at least, been our experience during years of gardening and talking to gardeners. And the uncommon, we felt, sometimes deserved inclusion among the unknowns, if it could add to the pleasure and satisfaction of many gardeners.

Because many readers may be looking in this book for some particular vegetable they enjoyed while abroad, we have carried each plant by the name these travelers were apt to have heard at the time. In the description, we have then given other names by which the vegetable is known. Mao gwa is also Chinese fuzzy gourd and wax gourd, for example, and other vegetables have five or six aliases. For a handy identification reference, see the list in chapter two, Some Gardening Basics, giving each plant's chapter name, botanical name, and any alternate names.

Some of these names led us into investigations as intriguing as a mystery thriller. Plants have changed their names as they scattered about the world and, in some cases, changed their employment. Say "gourd" to an American, and it summons up a picture of ornaments, containers, perhaps pipes (calabash), and sponges (luffa). But in the Orient the gourd is eaten, and the edible species are valued; see the chapter on cee gwa, vines of which are presently flourishing in our garden. The stir-fry recipe with cashew nuts, carried in that chapter, came from a Chinese friend.

We are indebted to many world-traveling friends, who filled gaps in our gardening and cooking experiences when we encountered certain exotic vegetables that deserved inclusion here but which we had not yet grown.

Because we happen to be better acquainted with vegetables of Europe and the Orient than of other parts of the globe, it is largely these we have dealt with here. Another factor is climate. We would have liked to include jicama, for instance, a large tuber we have enjoyed experimenting with in the kitchen, but it does not seem to thrive north of Central America. On the other hand, some of the daikon types—the Oriental radishes—bear a reasonable resemblance to jicama's taste and texture, and the daikon is not hard to grow in most of the United States.

Again, we were tempted to include bamboo for the sake of its succulent shoots. But the bamboos most productive of shoots are subtropical and are also hard to keep in bounds. We once had to rogue out an estimated 10,000 canes on a property we owned in the Gulf Coast South because they were taking over. Therefore, we bypassed bamboo but included Belgian endive, which, while not in the least related to bamboo, can sometimes be used in its place, and in many other delicious ways as well.

So, we wish you pleasure in the gardening and dining adventures between these covers. If you find even only one or two new plants you are glad to discover, we'll be pleased. And you may find sixty-one.

SOME GARDENING BASICS

SITE

The site of a garden is usually a take-it-or-leave-it choice. We do the best with what we have. Here we describe the best conditions—but don't be dismayed if you don't have all of them. Neither have we had them, during years of gardening in half a dozen widely differing regions of this country, and we have seldom felt deprived. Here are the important points to consider as to site.

Soil A fertile soil that can be easily raked into a fine seedbed is just right—a sandy loam. It doesn't let water sink away too rapidly, or run off, but it doesn't get soggy either. Most gardeners will have a soil on one side or the other of the ideal—more sandy or more clayey. Happily, the same medicine helps both problems—the addition of organic matter to the soil. We recommend getting it in the form of compost, which we'll discuss shortly. A soil analysis can tell you something of your soil's physical makeup, and also whether it lacks any nutrients plants will need. An analysis is probably most instructive if you are having trouble with one or more crops. Do-it-yourself kits for this are advertised in gardening magazines, and your county agricultural agent will know of soil-testing laboratories. Look under your county name in the telephone directory for the agent's number at the county seat.

For in-depth information on soils, a new book, *Don't Call It Dirt,* by Gordon Baker Lloyd (Bookworm Publishing Company, Ontario, CA 91761), thoroughly covers the garden-front.

Sun and Air   After the soil, the next items of importance for a good site are sun and air. Most plants want plenty of both. "Sun" means six or more hours of daily sunshine. "Air" means a site open to the breezes. If your garden gets much less than six hours of daily sunshine (cloudy days don't count, unless most of your days are cloudy), the best crops for you are leafy greens. You can also chance some root crops. But plants that grow fruits (e.g. Italian tomatoes, Oriental cucumbers, cee gwa, courgettes) or pods (dow gauk, fava beans, haricots) generally underproduce or don't produce at all with less than six hours of full sun. Our own policy is to take a chance when in doubt; but we do so knowing we're courting disaster. Success under those conditions, however, is sweet indeed.

Water   Water is the next point to consider. The rule of thumb for garden watering is: one inch of rain a week. If you don't get that much rain in any given week, make up the difference with water from the hose. So try to see that your garden site is located so as to make watering by hose possible. If you simply can't manage this, mulch the plants well and deep-water them by bucket. We go into mulching further along. The mulch-and-bucket system is work, but it grows vegetables. It was what we used with a big farm-garden and some smaller ones. After a time you learn to tell by a plant's looks when it needs the bucket.

Convenience   The next point in considering a garden site is your convenience. Some gardeners would put this item at the top of the list. A garden should be handily near the kitchen, which also locates it well for doing garden chores. When such a site is out of the question —as with a community garden or the cultivation of a neighborhood vacant lot—we'd vote to do it anyway, and have. But you do give up the convenience and also lose some of the satisfying rapport one has with a garden close to home.

Competition   Finally as to site, there is the matter of competition the garden will have from nearby plants. Trees are the commonest problem. A tree too close to the garden will shade the vegetables and will lap up all the garden's water and fertilizer it can get its roots on. If you can, locate your garden ten feet or more beyond the farthest reach of the tree's nearest branches. If you can't, just live with the problem. Trees are greedy but not lethal to vegetables (except black walnut trees, which have a depressing effect on tomatoes). Part of our present garden surrounds a fig tree, skirts an apple tree, and abuts hard on an English walnut; the vegetables are all producing, and the fruits and nuts prosper beyond reason.

COMPOST AND OTHER
FERTILIZERS

Compost is a soil conditioner and an exceptional mulch. We use it in both these ways but also regard it as the backbone of our fertilizing program when so used. This is because well-made compost contains up to 10 percent of the three most needed chemicals—nitrogen, phosphorus, and potassium—along with all or most of the other nutrients that plants must have.

In addition to compost, we most often fertilize with cottonseed meal, because it is generally available (farm feed stores sell it, as well as some garden suppliers), and it is strong where compost is light (nitrogen), and light where compost is strong (potassium). Soybean meal and linseed meal are good substitutes for cottonseed meal. In the vegetable chapters we indicate the amounts of fertilizer to use for each vegetable.

As to compost, it is a mixture of vegetative wastes decomposed by bacteria and fungi. We use a fast method of making compost, one developed by the University of California in the 1950s. Here's how:

First, you'll need two containers, each able to hold two-thirds or so of a cubic yard. These can be wooden bins 2½ feet square and 3 feet high. Or build a single one 5 feet long, 2½ feet wide, and 3 feet high, and divide it in two with a middle partition. The bins are open top and bottom. Another way is to bend a 10-foot piece of 3-foot-high wire fencing (rabbit wire will do) into a cylinder. Two of these will make satisfactory bins if you fasten three broomstick-type legs to each, evenly spaced around the inside, as supports, and then wrap the outside of each cylinder with plastic such as an old shower curtain.

To make compost, fill a bin with a mixture of about one part by volume of dryish organic wastes such as sawdust, straw, or dry leaves, and three parts of juicy stuffs such as grass clippings, tender prunings, chopped weeds, kitchen vegetable wastes. As you fill the bin, mix the materials rather than layering them. If the mixture feels about as damp as a squeezed sponge, don't add water. If it feels dryer than this, dampen it. Two or three days later, turn the mixture into the second bin with a spading fork, putting what was in the center on the sides this time. Add water if needed, and repeat this turning every two or three days. You'll notice that the compost becomes quite hot, rising to about 160° F. in the center of the pile. In about two weeks the compost should be ready to go to work as a dark, crumbly, and moist mixture.

STARTING PLANTS
AHEAD OF TIME

We seed plants in flats indoors for two reasons. One is to get a crop sooner by putting growing plants instead of seeds in the garden. Tender things that cold weather would kill, such as tomato seedlings, get a head start this way. The other reason for seeding in flats is that scarce garden space isn't filled with infant plants. This is more important in a small garden than a large one. Another point about starting plants ahead of time in flats is that you can protect them from pests more effectively than when they are in the open garden. And young plants are much more vulnerable to most scourges.

You can fill a flat with a commercial potting mixture and seed in that. Or you can make your own mixture. Equal parts of good garden soil, screened compost, and perlite or sharp sand make a satisfactory combination. Today there are also several brands of peat blocks or pots in which seeds can be sown. As the plants grow, their roots fill the peat, making later transplanting fast and easy on the plants.

A temperature of 70° F. is needed for germination for most plants. After germination, they grow better in flats at a temperature of 65° F., give or take two or three degrees. Grow them where they get light from a south or east window, and turn the flats daily or the plants will develop a permanent lean toward the light.

Before you move plants from indoors to the garden, give them airings outside for a couple of weeks to get them used to life outdoors. Start with an hour or so of airing (not in wind or hot sun), and increase it by an hour a day.

MULCHING

A mulch is anything laid on the soil around plants that improves growing conditions. We prefer compost for this purpose, but since there is never enough to go around, we and other gardeners also use such materials as wood shavings, leaves, shrub prunings, straw, and sawdust. Almost any organic matter available where one lives will do. It is a good idea to pull a mulch aside now and then to see if any pests are living happily underneath it. Also a thick mulch should be inspected to see if it is letting water through to the plant roots properly. "Thick" here means from 8 inches to a foot or two. A 1-inch mulch would be a thin one, and 3 or 4 inches is fairly average.

Plastic sheeting is being used by commercial growers for mulching and works well. We don't care for its looks in a garden, and there is a problem when water must be applied under the plastic.

PESTS

Different areas have different pest populations, and the way to see which pests may plague your garden is to talk to nearby gardeners. Like many gardeners today, we go light on pest killers, relying more on prevention. By this we mean frequent inspections of the garden to see if insect damage or disease is about, keeping the garden clear of trash, growing plants briskly. Caterpillars and some slow-moving bugs can be removed by hand and stepped on. Poison baits will kill many snails, slugs, and earwigs. A spray of dishwater-strength soapsuds or detergent solution, quickly followed by a plain water spray, can rid a plant of some pests and occasionally seems to act as a repellent to others. For some mysterious reason, the solution called compost tea also drives some pests away. To make it, let a spadeful of compost steep in a bucket of water for 30 minutes; drain off the water, dilute it with about six parts of water, and sprinkle it on plants being attacked. You don't have to follow up with plain water in this case. The treatment has worked for us with squash and some other plants.

A combination of rotenone and pyrethrum is a good wide-purpose pest killer, stomach poison, contact poison, and repellent, and is harmless to warm-blooded creatures.

Finally, there are the predatory insects. These devour legions of the pest insects and include the lacewing flies, wasps, rove beetles, hover flies, ground beetles, dragonflies, ladybugs, and spiders. Every garden has some of these good insects, one of nature's bounties and a blessing to us all.

NAMES BY WHICH THE PLANTS COVERED IN THIS BOOK ARE KNOWN

Adzuki bean, *Phaseolus angularis.*
Armenian cucumber, *Cucumis sativa.* Armenian Yard-Long cucumber.
Asparagus pea, *Psophocarpus tetragonolobus.* Goa bean.
Belgian endive, *Cichorium intybus.* Witloof chicory, succory, blueweed, coffeeweed.
Caraway, *Carum carvi.* Kummel.
Cardoon, *Cynara cardunculus.*
Cee gwa, *Luffa acutangula.* Chinese okra, strainer vine.
Celeriac, *Apium graveolens* var. *rapaceum.* Turnip-rooted celery.
Celtuce, *Lactuca sativa* var. *asparagina.* Asparagus lettuce.
Chervil, *Anthriscus cerefolium.*
Chinese cabbages, *Brassica pekinensis.* Pe-tsai. *B. chinensis.* Pac choi, pak choy, bok choy.

Chinese celery, *Apium graveolens.* Heung kunn.

Chinese chive, *Allium odoratum.*

Cilantro, *Coriandrum sativum.* Coriander, Chinese parsley, yuen sai.

Courgettes, *Cucurbita pepo.* Squashes.

Daikon, *Raphanus sativus* var. *longipinnatus.* Oriental radish, Japanese radish.

Doan gwa, *Benincasa hispida.* Chinese winter melon, wax gourd.

Dow gauk, *Vigna sesquipedalis.* Yard-long bean, asparagus bean.

Eschalot, *Allium ascalonicum.* Shallot.

Fava beans, *Vicia faba.* Broad beans, windsor beans, giant English beans, European beans, horse beans.

Fenugreek, *Trigonella foenum-graecum.* Helbeh.

Fetticus, *Valerianella locusta* var. *olitoria.* Vetticost, lamb's lettuce, mache, corn salad.

Fingerling potatoes, *Solanum tuberosum.* Salad potatoes, lady-finger potatoes.

Finnochio, *Foeniculum vulgare* var. *dulce.* Florence fennel, fennel.

Flageolets, *Phaseolus vulgaris.* French shell beans.

Foo gwa, *Momordica charantia.* Chinese bitter melon, bitter gourd.

Fraises des bois, *Fragaria vesca.* Strawberries of the woods, perpetual strawberries, Alpine strawberries.

French carrots, *Daucus carota sativa.*

Gai lohn, *Brassica alboglabra.* Chinese kale, Chinese broccoli.

Gobo, *Arctium lappa.* Edible burdock, edible goberon.

Hamburg parsley, *Petroselinum radicatum.* Turnip-rooted parsley.

Haricots, *Phaseolus vulgaris.* French snap beans.

Hinn choy, *Amaranthus gangeticus.* Amaranth, Joseph's coat, Chinese spinach.

Husk tomatoes, *Physalis pruinosa.* Strawberry tomato, ground cherry.

Indian mustards, *Brassica juncea.* Chinese mustard.

Italian beans, *Phaseolus vulgaris.* Italian green-pod bean.

Italian parsley, *Petroselinum crispum.* Flat-leaf parsley, plain-leaf parsley.

Italian tomatoes, *Lycopersicum esculentum.* Paste tomatoes.

Kale, *Brassica oleracea* var. *acephala.* Borecole, colewort.

Kohlrabi, *Brassica caulorapa.* Turnip cabbage, turnip-rooted cabbage, stem cabbage.

Leek, *Allium porrum.*

Mao gwa, *Benincasa hispida.* Chinese fuzzy gourd, wax gourd.

Mitsuba, *Cryptotaenia japonica.* Japanese parsley.

Orach, *Atriplex hortensis.* Mountain spinach, French spinach, sea purslane, butter leaves.

Oriental cucumbers, *Cucumis sativus.*

Oriental eggplants, *Solanum melongena.*

Oriental pumpkins, *Cucurbita pepo.*

Petits pois, *Pisum sativum.* French peas.

Radichetta, *Cichorium* species. Asparagus chicory, Italian chicory, Italian dandelion, ciccoria Catalogna.

Rocambole, *Allium sativum.* Sand leek, Spanish garlic, serpent garlic.

Roquette, *Eruca sativa.* Rocket.

Scorzonera, *Scorzonera hispanica.* Black salsify, black oyster plant.

Sea-kale, *Crambe maritima.* Scurvy grass.

Sesame, *Sesamum orientale.* Bene, benne, benny.

Shungiku, *Chrysanthemum coronarium.* Crown daisy, garland chrysanthemum, fragrant greens, chop suey greens.

Sicilian fennel, *Foeniculum vulgare* var. *piperitum.* Carosella.

Snow peas, *Pisum sativum.* Sugar peas, edible-podded peas.

Sorrel, *Rumex* species. Dock, sour dock, curled dock, patience, monk's rhubarb, garden sorrel.

Sparachetti, *Brassica oleracea italica.* Broccoli raab, broccoli-headed turnip, Italian turnip, rapine, rapone.

Upland cress, *Barbarea vulgaris.* Winter cress, bitter winter cress, rocket, yellow rocket. *B. verna.* Early cress, Belle Isle cress, scurvy-grass.

Welsh onions, *Allium fistulosum.* Ciboul, two-bladed onion, spring onion, bunching onion, Japanese bunching onion.

3

SOME COOKING BASICS

Most of the recipes appear in the vegetable chapters. Those in this chapter are here because they apply to more than one vegetable— sauces, for instance. A recipe title with an asterisk after it, e.g. bechamel sauce*, indicates that the recipe will be found here, in chapter three.

Throughout the book we have avoided complicated recipes, believing that the tastes of unusual and unfamiliar vegetables should not be masked by many other flavorings or by elaborate preparation.

We have also tried to avoid recipes that require ingredients most of us are unlikely to locate. When this is unavoidable, we suggest optional ingredients where possible.

COOKING TERMS
USED HERE

Sauté: to cook in a small amount of fat, uncovered.
Braise: to sauté first, then cover pan for final cooking.
Steam: to cook with moist heat from water that does not touch the food.
Stir-fry: to cook rapidly in a small amount of oil, uncovered, over high heat. In the Orient, stir-frying is done with small portions of food at a time for faster cooking, and the vegetables are cut so as to expose much of the interior flesh. With a stem of bok choy, for example, the cut should be a diagonal one, with the knife slanted. A cee gwa, which roughly resembles an oversize okra pod, might be cut lengthwise in halves and then quarters.

Poach: used in Oriental cooking, this is a fast parboiling in which small amounts of the vegetable are dropped into rapidly boiling water from one to five minutes, fished out, and the next batch dropped in. The water should not stop boiling at any time. For this cooking method the vegetable is usually cut to expose the least amount of interior flesh.

RECIPES

BECHAMEL SAUCE

3 tablespoons butter	1/2 teaspoon minced thyme
1 eschalot, minced	1 teaspoon minced parsley
1/2 small carrot, finely chopped	1/8 teaspoon sugar
2 tablespoons flour	1/8 teaspoon salt
1/2 cup rich chicken stock	1/4 teaspoon grated nutmeg
1/2 cup half-&-half or cream	1 teaspoon cognac (optional)

Melt butter in saucepan, add eschalot and carrot, simmer 5 minutes. Stir in flour to make a roux* and simmer another minute. Add liquids, increase heat, stir until sauce thickens. Lower heat, stir in seasonings. Strain before serving, if you wish. Makes a generous cupful.

MORNAY SAUCE

To make mornay sauce, add ½ cup grated Parmesan cheese to the amount of bechamel sauce the previous recipe yields. Stir in the cheese after straining the sauce. (Straining is traditional haute cuisine but is not imperative.)

HOLLANDAISE SAUCE

5 tablespoons butter	3 tablespoons boiling water
2 egg yolks	salt
1 tablespoon warm lemon juice	cayenne sauce

Melt butter in top of double boiler over just a little water, barely simmering. Remove from heat and beat in egg yolks. Return to heat and cook with almost constant stirring until mixture thickens. Stir in lemon juice, then the water, one tablespoon at a time. Season with a little salt and a dash of the cayenne sauce. If curdling occurs, stir in a little more boiling water. Makes about three-quarters of a cup.

VINAIGRETTE SAUCE

2 tablespoons lemon juice
3 tablespoons cider vinegar
1/3 cup olive oil
1/3 cup salad oil
1 teaspoon salt
1/8 teaspoon pepper

1/2 teaspoon dry mustard
1 teaspoon minced parsley
1 teaspoon minced tarragon
1 tablespoon finely chopped chives
1 tablespoon finely chopped capers

Mix all ingredients together and stir or shake well. Repeat stirring or shaking before using. Makes a generous cupful.

FRENCH DRESSING

1/2 teaspoon salt
1/2 teaspoon dry mustard
1/4 teaspoon sugar
1 garlic clove, peeled and split
2 teaspoons lemon juice

2 tablespoons white wine
  vinegar
1/4 cup olive oil
3/4 cup salad oil
sprig of basil (optional)

Put ingredients in the order listed in a pint jar. Cap the jar and shake well. Let understand overnight to blend flavors. If wanted for use at once, bruise basil before adding it and squeeze garlic through press.
   This dressing can be stored at ordinary room temperatures for use over a week. Makes about 1¼ cups.

CATHAY SAUCE

1/2 teaspoon ground ginger
1 tablespoon cornstarch
1 teaspoon dark molasses

2 tablespoons soy sauce
1 cup chicken stock, or half
  chicken, half beef stock

Combine ginger and cornstarch in small bowl. Stir in molasses and soy sauce. Bring stock to a simmer in saucepan. Stir a tablespoon of the stock into mixture in bowl until blended, then add to stock in saucepan. Cook over medium-low heat with occasional stirring until sauce becomes clear and slightly thickened. Makes a generous cupful.

BOUQUET GARNI

A small bunch of herbs used to flavor a dish while it is being cooked is called a bouquet garni—a French term that has come into general usage. The choice of herbs is flexible, and even a single herb may be considered a bouquet garni. Those most frequently employed are parsley, basil, thyme, savory, marjoram, celery leaves, and bay leaf. Whole cloves or peppercorns are sometimes included. The herbs are held together with a bit of string or are enclosed in a little piece of cloth. They can also be sandwiched in a finger-long piece of split leek whose waist is then tied with string. It is customary to discard a bouquet garni after use.

FINES HERBES

Unlike the tolerant bouquet garni, fines herbes are always supposed to be produced the same way: finely chopped (the term means "minced herbs") and of the same ingredients: fresh parsley, chives, tarragon, and chervil. You may, however, use as much or as little of each herb in your particular fines herbes as you please. The herbs are not removed from the finished dish as is the bouquet garni.

To the purist, dried herbs in fines herbes are unthinkable. This poses a wintertime problem that fines herbes lovers struggle with. But if you ask us, dried herbs are better than no herbs.

DUXELLES

This is a stock item in French cooking, a way of having on hand mushrooms for flavoring. You will need a pound of mushrooms, more or less, to end up with about a pint of duxelles.

3 tablespoons butter	1/4 teaspoon grated nutmeg
1 tablespoon olive oil	1 tablespoon minced parsley
2 eschalots, minced	salt and pepper
1 pound mushrooms, finely chopped	1 tablespoon cognac (optional)
1 tablespoon chicken stock	

Heat butter and oil in saucepan; add eschalots, mushrooms, and stock. Simmer 10 minutes with occasional stirring. Remove pan from heat and stir in the other ingredients. (We sometimes omit the salt and pepper, or use very little, to avoid overseasoning dishes to which the duxelles will be added.) Cool, and keep in covered jar in the re-frigerator. Two weeks is average storage life for us.

HERB BUTTERS

This popular seasoning is used to add flavoring, often near the end of the cooking time. Herbs frequently used are parsley, basil, thyme, marjoram, and tarragon.

Mince enough of a given herb to fill a ¼-cup measure. With the flat side of a broad knife work 8 tablespoons of butter soft on a dinner plate. Add the minced herb and continue working the butter until the two are well-blended. Toward the end of the working, add ½ teaspoon of lemon juice.

Store the herb butter in the refrigerator in a covered jar. It will easily keep for a week or longer.

The amount added to a dish depends on the strength of the herb. In general, parsley and tarragon can be used more freely than basil, thyme, and marjoram.

CHINESE GRAVY

For binding and flavoring many Oriental dishes, a "gravy" or sauce is made of cornstarch stirred into cold water to a cream consistency, to which is added soy sauce. The proportions are approximately 1 table-spoon of cornstarch to ¼ cup of water and 1-2 tablespoons of soy sauce. Some cooks prefer a mild vegetable stock in place of the water. To use the gravy, stir it into the dish being cooked, a little at a time, until the desired consistency is reached. This is done shortly before serving.

An alternative recipe employs flour as the thickening agent. Brown 3 tablespoons of flour in a saucepan, stirring. Stir in 3 table-spoons of fat (butter, bacon drippings, or lard). Slowly add ⅓ cup of beef stock and 2 tablespoons of soy sauce, stirring constantly until gravy is smooth and thick.

TOASTED SESAME SEEDS

Put ¼ cup of sesame seeds in a skillet and cook over low heat. Stir frequently because the seeds burn easily. Salt is sometimes added, the rate being ¼ teaspoon for this amount of seeds. A little butter or oil can be used instead, although this makes the stirring a little more trouble, the seeds being inclined to cling to each other. *After seeds are golden brown, they can be added at once to another dish for flavoring, but are frequently crushed at this point to increase flavor. This can be done with mortar and pestle or in a bowl with the back of a heavy spoon.*

TEMPURA BATTER

Mix a beaten egg yolk, 2 cups of chilled water, and enough flour to make a thin batter—about 1½ cups. To use the batter, dip pieces of food in it, shake off excess batter, and drop the pieces in deep oil heated to 375° F. for about 2 minutes, turning them halfway through. Remove when lightly browned.

(For a beer batter, see the scorzonera chapter.)

ROUX

A roux is a fat-and-flour mixture used to thicken a sauce. To make it, melt the fat—butter is most favored—stir in the flour, and cook over low heat for 1-2 minutes with frequent stirring. Equal parts of fat and flour are usually used—1 tablespoon of each to make a cup of a thin sauce, 2 tablespoons of each for a cup of medium sauce, and 3 tablespoons of each for a cup of thick sauce. Some cooks add the liquid to the roux gradually; some add it all at once. Both methods work. The important part is the stirring, which must be almost continuous until the sauce thickens, to get a smooth product.

To make a brown roux, sometimes called for in the case of a dark sauce, put the flour in the saucepan first and cook it over low heat with frequent stirring until it browns. Then proceed as above.

CROUTONS

Trim crusts from slices of bread and cut slices into enough cubes to fill a 1-cup measure. Put cubes in skillet, sprinkle with 1 tablespoon of olive oil, and cook over low heat, shaking skillet now and then, until cubes are crisp outside and lightly browned. Use within an hour or two.

THE VEGETABLES

⌁ ADZUKI BEAN — Orient ⌁

This little bean from the Orient prefers cool summer nights, so if that is the pattern of your climate—as it is in coastal California, some parts of the Northwest, and in high altitudes—try planting adzuki beans if you also have a frost-free growing season four months long. Botanically *Phaseolus angularis,* adzukis are not soy beans but are related to our snap and lima beans, and are also annuals. Adzukis grow in the bush form, about 2 feet tall, and are good bearers of fairly short green pods. Culture is the same as for snap beans: Seed them when the weather turns mild, in a sunny spot, after digging a 4-inch layer of compost into the soil. If your soil is alkaline, it will pay to dig in peat moss or sawdust at the rate of one bucketful to about 10 feet of row. This class of beans likes a soil pH between 5.5 and 6.5. When the plants are up and growing well, thin them so they are 8 inches apart. A compost mulch after the first three or four weeks of growth is in order.

Johnny, Metro Myster, and Thompson & Morgan list adzuki beans.

Adzuki beans can be eaten pod and all if picked young and tender. Cook them as you would snap beans. Older beans can be shelled out. They can also be allowed to dry and then shelled out for winter use. For drying instructions, see the flageolets section. Adzukis have a name for being rich in minerals, and their wide use in Asia suggests good nutritional levels. They are sweet and often used in cakes and other desserts in Asia and are said to have a high (20 percent) protein content. They are small and round, usually reddish.

Adzukis are one of the beans favored for sprouting, a process that adds nutritional value. Use dried adzukis for this purpose. See the fenugreek section for a sprouting procedure.

⌒ ARMENIAN CUCUMBER — Europe, Orient ⌒

This cucumber is also called the Armenian Yard-Long cucumber, as it does get fairly long, although 2 feet is about its ultimate length. It is also curvy, not a desirable characteristic, but this is forgiven it for its excellent flavor, meatiness, and crispness. Skin color is light green. Botanically it is *Cucumis sativa,* as are other cucumbers, and it is an annual.

Culture is that given for cee gwa. Sources of Armenian cucumber seed are Kitazawa and Nichols.

ARMENIAN CUCUMBER WITH SOUR CREAM

This is an excellent side dish to serve with fish.

1 Armenian cucumber	1/2 cup commercial sour cream
1/2 teaspoon lemon juice	freshly ground pepper

Peel cucumber and slice into silver-dollar-thick rounds into a bowl. Stir lemon juice into sour cream, and blend with cucumber slices by gentle stirring and lifting. Chill for an hour or longer. Serve in small sauce dishes, topped with pepper.

⌒ ASPARAGUS PEA — Europe ⌒

This little annual legume, popular in England, has one of the longer botanical names: *Psophocarpus tetragonolobus.* It is also known as goa bean and came from Africa. It develops a neat bush-type of plant about 12 inches high and bears heavily. Culture is the same as for the more familiar peas: Seed in compost-enriched soil in spring, about April 1 in the Midwest, in an open site.

Asparagus peas are picked quite young, when pods are no more than 1 inch long. (Mature ones grow to 8 inches or longer.) The harvesting begins about fifty days after seed is planted. Pods are four-angled and will be produced for two months or longer if regularly picked. The plant's tuberous roots are also edible, and it is sometimes grown solely for this crop. Seed is carried by Park, and Thompson & Morgan.

Some say the asparagus pea tastes something like mushrooms, while others seem to discover an artichoke flavor. The usual preparation is simple: *Braise the whole pods in butter or in butter and vegetable oil until fork-tender, and season lightly with salt.*

ASPARAGUS PEA SALAD

2 cups asparagus peas	1/2 cup croutons*
1/2 cup French dressing*	paprika
lettuce leaves	

Steam asparagus peas tender. Transfer them to a bowl, pour dressing evenly over them, cover with plastic, and chill in refrigerator, stirring gently two or three times so that all the peas are well-coated. To serve, arrange peas on lettuce in salad bowl, and sprinkle with the croutons, and with enough paprika to show color. Makes four portions.

BELGIAN ENDIVE – Europe

So few gardeners grow the solid little creamy-white crisp sprouts called Belgian endive that doing so will exalt you into a kind of gardeners' hall of fame in the eyes of your beholders. This is because this delicacy is almost entirely imported from Belgium and France (it is also known as French endive). It is one of the more expensive vegetables at two dollars a pound or so.

Aside from taking about half a year from start to finish, growing Belgian endive *(Cichorium intybus)* is not difficult nor is it finicky. You do the job in two steps.

First you grow a crop of witloof chicory in well-spaded, compost-enriched soil, seeding it in mid-May or in June. Earlier seeding in all but very short-season climates is not advisable because the chicory will bolt to seed if given too much growing time. Thin the plants 6 inches apart. They look something like cos lettuce, and their leaves can furnish an agreeably bitter green, but let them keep all or most of them to nourish the roots. These take about four months to grow, and the plants can use a side-dressing of wood ashes when half-grown.

When fall comes, dig the roots after cutting off all but an inch of the leafy tops. Bury the roots in a box of dry sand and store in a

Belgian endives, sprouted from wit-loof chicory roots in wintertime, look something like tightly rolled little cos lettuces. They are crisp and delicious in salads. W. ATLEE BURPEE CO.

cool place.

To grow the Belgian endives, you sprout the roots, a batch at a time, in a cellar or any place with a cool house temperature. A nail keg is about the right depth for this sprouting procedure, but any wooden box about 18 inches deep will do. Bore a few holes in the bottom for drainage, and cover the holes with charcoal chunks. Then put 10 inches of earth in the box. Next, trim enough off the bottoms of a dozen or so chicory roots to make them uniformly about 7 inches long. Push them firmly into the earth in the box, spacing them about 3 inches apart. Their trimmed tops should be slightly below the soil surface.

Now moisten the earth and cover the roots with 8 inches of sawdust. Wet the sawdust to a damp-sponge moistness. Cover the box with a few thicknesses of damp newspaper.

Check the sawdust a few times a week, keeping it moist. In about a month, sprouts will start breaking the sawdust surface. Harvest them as soon as they do, cutting them off at the tops of the roots. It takes a week or so for all to sprout to harvestable size.

If you have enough roots, you can start a new box of them sprouting every week or ten days for a continuous supply.

There is another way to grow Belgian endives if you live in a mild climate. Don't dig the roots at all, but just trim the leafy tops as described. Then box the bed with boards 12 inches wide. Spread 2 inches of earth inside the box and follow with 8 inches of sawdust. Wet the sawdust and keep it damp but not soggy. You might wonder how you'll cope if the harvest all comes in at once, but we find that the sprouts space their emergence fairly well. And if you do get six or eight sprouts in one day, they keep well in the refrigerator.

Incidentally, this plant is a perennial, and if it were not dug for its roots, it would go on growing year after year. In fact it has done this in many parts of the country so that it has become a wild plant.

Americans who know Belgian endive are most likely to serve it raw in salads, but this epicurean vegetable is often cooked in Europe. The tightly rolled heads can be simmered in water or vegetable stock until fork-tender, lightly salted, and served dressed with an herb butter* or with melted butter and a whisper of nutmeg.

Sometimes a white sauce is used in place of the butter, in which case the cooked endives may be arranged in a shallow baking dish, covered with the sauce and a sprinkle of grated Parmesan cheese. Bake about 10 minutes in a 400° F. oven.

BELGIAN ENDIVES EDAM

4 cooked Belgian endives	salt
4 tablespoons melted butter	4 slices Edam cheese
2 eschalots, minced	

Arrange endives in a shallow baking dish. Mix melted butter with eschalots and pour over endives, coating each. Salt lightly. Place a slice of cheese on each endive. Bake at 275° F. until cheese has melted. Then slide the dish under broiler until cheese topping is golden brown. Makes four portions.

BELGIAN SALAD

4 cooked Belgian endives	lettuce leaves
1 recipe vinaigrette sauce*	

Marinate endives in the sauce for 2 hours or longer, in refrigerator. Serve endives on lettuce in salad bowl, topped with the sauce. Makes four portions.

⌒ CARAWAY – Europe ⌒

Botanically *Carum carvi,* caraway is thought to have originated in Western Asia, and its seeds have been used by mankind for thousands of years to flavor foods. A biennial, it produces its seed crop the second season, so seed it in late summer (seeds are slow to germinate,

Grown mainly for its seeds, used as a flavoring, caraway's attractive ferny foliage is also good to eat, as is its root, which can be cooked like a carrot. J. A. DEMONCHAUX CO.

like parsley), and thin plants to 8 inches apart. They are hardy in temperate climates and will produce a seed crop the next summer, usually in early midsummer. Mature plants are 3 feet tall. Although not a demanding plant, caraway prefers its soil sandy and with a pH of about 6.0, which is fairly acid.

Gather seed clusters when they are dry, and store them in paper grocery bags until seeds shake out. The seeds hold their flavor well when stored in capped containers.

Look under herb listings in seed catalogs for caraway.

Caraway seeds are used to flavor rye bread, some sauces, pastries, and so on. They make an interesting addition to cole slaw. A pinch of the seeds is a nice and different touch in a beef stew.

The thready fernlike leaves and young shoots of caraway can also be eaten in salads or put into soups and stews.

Even the caraway root is edible. Cooked in any way carrots are cooked, it has a mild creamlike flavor.

⌒ CARDOON – Europe ⌒

The cardoon, *Cynara cardunculus,* is an older relative of the globe artichoke, and the two plants have a strong family resemblance, being large handsome thistles with deeply lobed, gray-green leaves. Both are perennials. The cardoon is grown for its heavy leaf stalks, which form a bunch, like celery, and are blanched by gathering them together with a length of twine and wrapping the bunch with paper. This is done in the fall, and blanching takes three or four weeks. The bunch is then harvested by cutting it off at root top, taking a bit of root with it.

Cardoons are easily grown from seed sown during early spring in compost-enriched soil. In northern areas, start plants indoors, sowing seed in flats six to eight weeks before warm weather is due.

Partial shade is acceptable, and plants should stand about 2 feet apart. Like globe artichokes, cardoons need plenty of moisture, and they do their best in cool, mild climates. In cold climates they need a heavy mulch for winter protection.

Allow a few cardoon flowers to form their big bronzy-golden seed heads, then cut them, taking a good length of the strong stem. They make a splendid everlasting flower for a winter arrangement.

Cardoon seed is carried by Comstock, de Giorgi, Gurney, Hudson, le Jardin, and Nichols.

In ancient Rome, young leaves and stalks of cardoon were eaten as salad, and in fact the plant was as popular with second-century Romans, historians say, as lettuce and beans are with us today.

The heavy roots of cardoons are also edible and can be cooked like carrots or parsnips if you are willing to sacrifice the plant for this purpose.

To prepare cardoon stalks for cooking, pare off the spines along the stalk edges (some varieties are almost without spines) and the outer skin. A potato peeler is a good tool for this. Then cut stalks into pieces and steam or simmer them until fork-tender, which takes about 10 minutes.

CARDOONS WITH GARLIC SAUCE

An Italian way of serving pre-cooked cardoons—and also for use with globe artichokes as a dip for the leaves in place of hollandaise sauce*, which is also excellent—is to make a sauce of garlic and butter, flavored with anchovies. For most American tastes, suitable proportions are ½ cup of melted butter into which is stirred 1 teaspoon of anchovy paste; a garlic clove is then squeezed into the mixture through a press, and dry vermouth or lemon juice is sometimes added. Except for melting the butter, the sauce is not cooked.

CARDOON CASSEROLE

3 cups peeled and trimmed cardoon stalks cut into 1-inch pieces	1/8 teaspoon salt
	4 tablespoons melted butter
	1/2 cup freshly grated
vegetable stock	Romano cheese

Simmer cardoon pieces in stock until barely tender. Drain, put cardoon in shallow casserole. Add salt, drizzle melted butter over cardoon, and sprinkle with cheese. Bake in preheated 350° F. oven about 20 minutes or until cheese bubbles. Makes four portions.

CARDOONS WITH GREEN ONIONS

4 cups peeled and trimmed
  cardoon stalks cut into
  1-inch pieces
1/2 cup water
1 tablespoon garlic vinegar

2 green onions, chopped
2 tablespoons olive oil
1/2 cup rich chicken stock
salt and pepper

Cook cardoon pieces fork-tender in the water and garlic vinegar, covered. Add a little more water if needed.

In skillet, simmer onions in oil until soft. Add stock and the drained cardoon. Simmer, stirring, until cardoon has absorbed most of the stock. Season with salt and pepper. Makes four portions.

CEE GWA – Orient

Cee gwa is the Chinese name for an edible gourd that bears ridged fruits 6 inches long and 2 inches wide, tapering to a point and resembling large okra pods. For this reason, the plant is also called Chinese okra, a completely misleading name. Botanically it is a cucurbit, *Luffa acutangula,* and a close relative, by the way, of the gourd that grows the well-known luffa sponges. Both are annuals.

As you might suppose, cee gwa is a heat lover, needing about three months of warm weather to start fruiting. Plants can be started indoors and set out when weather is mild, 6 inches apart in soil enriched with compost and with a pound of cottonseed meal worked into each 15 feet of row. This row can be along a fence or trellis, for plants grow to 10 or more feet. Tie the vines along the support horizontally when they reach the top.

Keep the plants well-watered, and give them a mulch of compost after they are growing well.

Harvest fruits young, as old ones become fibrous. In fact, fully mature ones are employed as scrubbers and are handy for cleaning flower pods. For this purpose, let some fruits turn brown on the vine, cut them off, and dry them in the sun. Then cut off the ends, remove seeds, and soak off the skin.

Cee gwa is carried by Tsang & Ma.

Cee gwa is the Chinese name for this edible gourd, also called Chinese okra because its ribbed shape resembles an okra pod. Cee gwa fruits are eaten when about 6 inches long and are excellent stir-fried. TSANG & MA INTERNATIONAL

Prepare cee gwa for·cooking by slicing off the ridges and both ends.

Cee gwa can be eaten raw, as in a salad. For this purpose, slice it like a cucumber into thin rounds.

For deep frying, cut cee gwa into finger-size pieces, coat with tempura batter*, and cook at 375° F. until golden brown.

CEE GWA WITH CASHEWS

This is a fast dish and a very good one.

2 tablespoons oil	2 cups cooked chicken chunks
2 cee gwa prepared for cooking	1/2 cup broken cashew nuts

Heat oil in wok or heavy skillet. Cut cee gwa into small chunks and stir-fry in the oil 2-3 minutes. Add chicken and nuts, stir-fry another minute.

CEE GWA WITH SNOW PEAS

2 tablespoons oil	1/2 cup whole button
1 cup chopped cee gwa	mushrooms
1 cup slivered snow peas	1/3 cup Cathay sauce*

Heat oil in heavy skillet, add vegetables, and stir-fry 4-5 minutes. Add sauce, stir-fry ½ minute more.

In the Orient a soup is made by dropping chunks of cee gwa into a clear soup such as a consomme during the last few minutes of cooking.

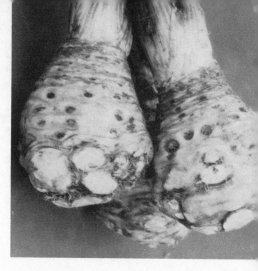

Little known in American gardens, popular in Europe, the knobby root of celeriac is one of the good winter vegetables. It keeps well and tastes like a nut-flavored celery. JOSEPH HARRIS CO.

An early nineteenth-century English botanical writer, William Roxburgh, said of cee gwa that when boiled, dressed with butter, and seasoned with salt and pepper, it was almost as good as green peas. Coming from an Englishman, this was praise indeed.

⟵ CELERIAC – Europe ⟶

Although close kin to the popular celery, celeriac is a stranger to most American kitchens and gardens. Few cooks know what to do with the bulbous root—which is the part of the plant eaten—of this vegetable Humpty-Dumpty. The taste is that of celery with nutlike overtones, thoroughly good and well worth your attention. Celeriac's botanical name is *Apium graveolens* var. *rapaceum*. It is a biennial grown as an annual.

Celeriac takes the same care as celery and requires the same four months to mature. See the section on Chinese celery for culture. But like celery, celeriac can be harvested ahead of time if you can't wait. Given all the time it wants, celeriac grows to about the size of a grapefruit.

To store celeriac, dig the mature root, cut off all but an inch of the top, and keep it in a cool room. It will remain in good condition all winter.

There is scant choice of varieties, but a number of seedsmen list Alabaster celeriac, or Giant Prague.

Celeriac is prepared for cooking by washing and peeling. It can be cooked whole, but since nearly all dishes call for slicing or cubing, this is done before cooking and shortens cooking time.

SIMMERED CELERIAC

This recipe for celeriac is Greek.

1 large celeriac peeled and cut
  into 1/2-inch cubes
1/2 cup water
1/2 cup chicken stock
1/2 cup tokay wine or dry
  vermouth

4 thin slices of lemon
1/8 teaspoon grated nutmeg
1/8 teaspoon salt
2 tablespoons butter

Put celeriac into saucepan with the water, bring to a boil, simmer until celeriac is fork-tender. Add all other ingredients except butter, and simmer 10 minutes. Add butter, and serve when butter has melted. Makes four portions.

An old German way of preparing celeriac is to peel it, slice it, cook it in water until tender, then steep the slices in vinegar, and chill them.

PICKLED CELERIAC

This is a European way of preparing celeriac.

1 large celeriac, about 1 pound
1/2 cup cider vinegar
1/4 cup water
2 peppercorns

2 cloves
1/8 teaspoon salt
1/2 teaspoon sugar
small bay leaf

Peel celeriac, cut into eighths lengthwise, and cut these pieces in half crosswise. Steam until just tender. Transfer to bowl. Prepare pickling liquid by simmering remaining ingredients together for 5 minutes. Pour immediately over celeriac, cover bowl, and when cool put into refrigerator for a few days before using.

⟿ CELTUCE — Orient ⟿

If you have ever tasted the juicy crispness of the inner core of a bolting lettuce stem, no doubt you forgave the plant for deciding to go to seed. Cut into a salad, the stem rivals a lettuce heart in taste and texture. The reason for this preamble to the subject of celtuce is that celtuce is a form of lettuce, both being *Lactuca sativa*. Furthermore,

Celtuce is a kind of lettuce grown mostly for its large and succulent main stem. It is good raw or cooked. The big lettucelike leaves can be cooked as greens. W. ATLEE BURPEE CO.

celtuce specializes in growing a stem. It is a large and succulent stem that goes happily into salads and is also at home in Oriental dishes. Like lettuce, celtuce is an annual.

Not surprisingly, celtuce is grown the same as lettuce, although in our experience celtuce is not as willing a grower. Seed it in early spring in compost-rich soil that is on the acid side, about a pH 6.0. Spading in some sawdust will help with acidity. Keep soil moist, and mulch with compost. Celtuce matures its stalk in three months.

Burpee, which introduced celtuce from China, lists it, as do Field, Gurney, Nichols, Stokes, and Thompson & Morgan.

Harvest celtuce by cutting it off at ground level. Strip off the leaves, which are not of salad quality but can be cooked like chard, and peel the stem.

The celtuce stem tastes something like globe artichoke to some. Others variously describe it as tasting like lettuce, celery, asparagus, squash, or chard. A vegetable for all people.

A good Occidental way to prepare celtuce is to braise ½-inch chunks of it in butter until tender, then serve them topped with mornay sauce* and a light snow of grated Romano cheese.

In the Orient, celtuce cut into ¼-inch pieces on the diagonal is stir-fried with shrimps and finely chopped Chinese celery, then served with a topping of toasted sesame seeds.*

Another stir-fry combination is: ¼-inch slices of celtuce, chopped mushrooms, and thinly sliced ginger root. This is seasoned lightly with salt and pepper.

Two-inch lengths of celtuce are poached (see chapter three for procedure), then sliced and served with a dash of soy sauce and a sprinkle of peanut oil.

⌒ CHERVIL – Europe ⌒

We are including chervil because it is far less known in American gardens and kitchens than some other widely useful herbs, although chervil has been long esteemed in Europe. And chervil is an essential in the flavoring of fines herbes.*

Chervil, *Anthriscus cerefolium,* is an annual and a willing grower. Seed it in spring in a well-prepared seed bed in sun or partial shade. It can also be seeded in late summer or fall in mild climates. Don't transplant it. Chervil grows to about 12 inches high, but some leaves can be cropped earlier, allowing more to be formed. We find it best to make two or three successive sowings a month apart, as plants get leggy when older. Spacing of 8 or 9 inches is often recommended, but chervil will take a good deal more crowding.

Like garden cress, which it looks like, chervil comes in both plain-leaf and curled-leaf varieties, but the curled one is more easily found and listed by several seedsmen.

For centuries chervil was grown in European gardens as a salad plant, and a little of it is an agreeable addition when chopped into a lettuce salad.

Chervil was so popular long ago as a seasoning herb in soup that it was said to have been among the ingredients in almost every

This Chinese cabbage is one of the heading, pe-tsai types. Some varieties are chunky like this one, about 10 inches high, and others are nearly twice as tall but not so wide. TSANG & MA INTERNATIONAL

French and Dutch soup. The young leaves do give soups and also stews a pleasant flavor that to some people most nearly resembles that of parsley. We think chervil tastes more like tarragon.

Chervil is sometimes added to potato salad as a seasoning, and it also looks attractive. Chop it finely for this purpose. We give a good potato salad recipe in the fingerling potatoes section.

CHINESE CABBAGES – Orient

Botanists tell us that Chinese cabbages are mustards. Cabbages and mustards are members of the same genus, *Brassica*. Chinese cabbages are annuals. After centuries of crossbreeding, there is inevitable confusion, but it is more of botanical than of gardening concern.

Most American gardeners probably know, at least by sight, the heading (pe-tsai) varieties of Chinese cabbage. Michihli is a tall one, about 18 inches high, and Wong Bok is a blocky one, 10 inches or so tall. The pe-tsai species is *Brassica pekinensis* and now includes many hybrids. Stokes lists three hybrid Wong Bok types that are said to take a good deal of hot weather and store well. Most U.S. seed houses carry some heading Chinese cabbages.

The loose-leaf Chinese cabbages, *Brassica chinensis,* are less well-known outside the Orient. They merit attention, and in our eyes are most worthwhile garden residents. Japanese seedsmen call them white celery mustards, but in American seed catalogs they are found listed among Chinese cabbages under their type name, bok choy, or as pac choi, pak choy, etc. Burpee carries a variety they call Crispy

Choy. Whatever name is used, the plants look a good deal like chard, having attractive medium-green leaves with strong white or greenish-white midribs. And also like chard, the outer leaves can be harvested one by one rather than harvesting the whole plant in the case of a late planting for fall use. Spring plantings are harvested as entire plants because most Chinese cabbages quickly bolt to seed when warm weather approaches.

Tsang & Ma carry a bok choy variety called Choy Sum. Its leaves are smaller than other bok choys and slightly sweeter. They recommend that the entire plant be harvested at its peak of growth, which is about 12 inches.

We find that the Chinese cabbages we have grown do best as fall crops from a late summer seeding, for they require short days and cool weather. They dislike transplanting, so permanently seed them in the garden in compost-enriched soil with a pound of cottonseed meal worked into 20 feet of row. Space plants 12 inches apart. The heading types mature in about twelve weeks but can be harvested sooner. The loose-leaf types mature in seven to nine weeks.

Chinese cabbage is delicately flavored and is cooked quickly. With a heading type, cut enough off the bottom to separate the leaves. They can then be coarsely chopped, dropped into boiling water, and cooked for a minute uncovered and another minute covered.

KIM CHEE

In Korea a kind of quick sauerkraut called kim chee is made of the heading Chinese cabbages.

Coarsely chop a head of Michihli or Wong Bok, sprinkle with 2 tablespoons of table salt, and mix well in a large bowl. Let it rest 20 to 30 minutes, stirring twice during this time. Then transfer cabbage to a large vessel and fill with cold water. Stir briefly and drain. Repeat this rinsing. Return cabbage to bowl and sprinkle with 1 tablespoon salt, add 3 green onions chopped coarsely, a garlic clove squeezed through press, and ½ teaspoon cayenne sauce. Stir mixture well, press down firmly, and add water to barely cover. Let ferment at a cool room temperature for a few days, covered with sheet plastic. It will increase in acidity each day and should be stored in refrigerator when the flavor is satisfactory, or it can be used at once. Refrigerated, it will keep 10 days. It can be used in any sauerkraut recipe.

Its mild but distinctive taste makes the loose-leaf Chinese cabbage, bok choy type, a nice salad plant. Or the leaves can be cooked as described for the heading types, or in a minimum of water, covered.

In China, however, stir-frying is often preferred for bok choys, sometimes in combination with shrimps, as in the following dish.

BOK CHOY SHRIMP

1 bok choy
1/4 cup oil
1 cup cleaned fresh
  shrimp
2 tablespoons soy sauce
1 tablespoon minced Chinese
  chives
cooked rice

Strip leaves from bok choy stems. Cut stems on the diagonal into pieces ¼ inch wide. Stir-fry them in the heated oil 2-3 minutes. Add shrimps and continue stir-frying 2-3 more minutes. Chop leaves medium coarse, add to stems and shrimps, and stir-fry another 1-2 minutes. Flavor with soy sauce, stir in Chinese chives, and serve at once over rice. Makes four to six portions.

BOK CHOY AND BEEF

2 tablespoons peanut oil
1/2 pound beef cut in thin
  strips
4 cups rinsed and shredded bok
  choy leaves stripped from stems
pepper
2 tablespoons soy sauce
1/4 cup toasted sesame
  seeds*

Heat oil in wok or heavy skillet, add beef, and stir-fry until beef changes color. Remove beef, add bok choy, stir-fry 3 minutes. Stir meat into bok choy, season with sprinkle of pepper and with soy sauce, remove from heat, and serve sprinkled with sesame seeds. Makes four portions.

GINGER CHOY SUM

Tsang & Ma recommend stir-frying 2-inch pieces of the bok-choy variety Choy Sum with black mushrooms and a few slices of ginger root. Thinly sliced fresh mushrooms can be used instead.

In the Orient, bok choy is dried for off-season use, as in soups. To dry it, cut leaves from stems, blanch leaves in boiling water for 2 minutes, and drain. Spread leaves, without overlapping, to dry in the sun or in the oven on cooky sheets covered with plastic wrap. Set oven at 130° F. The leaves are dried when crisp, and should be stored in closed plastic bags. To use the leaves soak them in water or stock 1 or 2 hours, and add to soup.

⌐ CHINESE CELERY — Orient ⌐

The Chinese call their celery heung kunn and especially prize it as a flavoring. Botanically it is the same species as our familiar celery, *Apium graveolens,* but the Chinese variety does not form a bunch. To borrow a lettuce term, Chinese celery is a lose-leaf type, which makes it easier to harvest single ribs as needed. Celery is a biennial grown as an annual.

Chinese celery is ready to begin harvesting about ten weeks after seeding, when the plant is about a foot tall. Young ribs are preferred, as older ones lose their crisp tenderness.

All celery demands rich soil and plenty of watering. You can directly seed Chinese celery in the garden in spring. It prefers partial shade. Start by spading in a 4-inch layer of compost. Then work a fertilizer such as cottonseed meal into the seed bed at the rate of a pound to 10 feet of row. Wet the soil well, seed thinly, and cover seeds lightly with potting soil. Then spread a sheet of black plastic over the bed and sprinkle it with about ½-inch layer of earth. This anchors the plastic and also keeps it from overheating the seeds if the sun should be too hot during germination. In about a week, check under an edge of the plastic and remove it as soon as sprouting starts.

Chinese celery is grown for flavoring, like an herb, and does not develop sizable ribs. TSANG & MA INTERNATIONAL

Two weeks later, thin plants to 6 inches apart. When they are half-grown, mulch with compost.

Tsang & Ma list Chinese celery.

Chinese celery has a more concentrated flavor than our celery and is chopped into many dishes much in the way parsley is used in Western cooking.

For stir-frying as a vegetable in its own right, Chinese celery is cut into ½-inch to 1½-inch pieces, including leaves, and is combined with beef or lamb.

Another stir-fry dish suggests combinations of thinly sliced ingredients such as Chinese celery, water chestnuts, mushrooms, bamboo shoots, onions, and meats such as pork, beef, lamb, chicken, or duck. Tsang & Ma give the Chinese name of this dish as sil chow, meaning "little delicate mixtures." It is thickened with Chinese gravy.*

Cut into very thin strips lengthwise and then chilled in ice water, Chinese celery becomes a garnish in bowls of soup.

CHINESE CHIVES – Orient

Plant Chinese chives once and you'll have them from then on, for this onion relative, *Allium odoratum* apparently, is a perennial like the other chives we all know, *A. schoenoprasum.* But there the resemblance ends. Chinese chive leaves are flat, not tubular, and they

Except for having flat leaves instead of tubular ones, Chinese chives look like other chives. The flavor of the Chinese kind, however, most resembles that of garlic. TSANG & MA INTERNATIONAL

do not have a mild onion flavor but taste authoritatively of garlic and can be used in place of it.

Chinese chives take all season to grow to a usable size, about 6 inches tall, and are best seeded in pots. They can stay in pots or be moved to a permanent place in the garden. They like their soil moist and rich but will get along with whatever is offered.

A mulch for winter protection is good in cold climates, but in most areas the roots will winter over without protection, sprouting anew in the spring.

Like other chives, these can be increased by digging the clumps in early spring and separating into several small clumps by pulling them gently apart. Chinese chive seed is carried by Grace, le Jardin, Nichols, and Tsang & Ma.

Overcooking will make Chinese chives stringy. Chop them finely and treat them as a seasoning, adding them to a dish the last minute or so of cooking.

The blossom buds of Chinese chives are also an article of food in China. To use them, cut buds before flowers open, taking some stem too. Like the chive leaves, the buds can be a salad ingredient, added to a stir-fry dish, or added to scrambled eggs during their cooking. Buds can be used whole or chopped.

CILANTRO — South and Central America, Orient, Europe

Usually listed in seed catalogs as coriander, this annual herb is one of the ancient ones, mentioned in the Bible (Numbers 11:7): "And the

manna was as coriander seed." Coriander is called cilantro in Mexico and is known as Chinese parsley or yuen sai in the Orient. Its botanical name is *Coriandrum sativum.*

The flavor of the fresh leaf is considerably stronger than the Italian parsley it resembles. Cilantro grows to 6 inches in two months or less from a spring or late summer seeding and eventually to as high as 3 feet. Space plants 6 inches apart by thinning, as they do not transplant easily. Cilantro will do well in average garden soil and will accept part shade.

Harvest seeds by pruning off the fruiting clusters when they dry and turn brown. If left on the plant too long, seeds will scatter. Store them in a dry place at room temperature for use as a seasoning.

Several seed houses list cilantro, usually among herbs, under the name coriander.

When used for flavoring, cilantro seeds are crushed or put through a pepper grinder to release the somewhat orangelike flavor. This flavor is given to dishes, such as a Mexican one of fresh pork cubes simmered with tomatoes, by soaking the crushed seeds in hot water, then adding the water only to the pork dish.

To give a Latin touch to chicken soup, finely chop enough cilantro leaves to provide a pinch per serving. Add it to the soup during the last 30 minutes of cooking, along with a ball of tomato paste (see recipe in the Italian tomatoes section) softened in a little hot water.

PORTUGUESE CILANTRO SOUP

6 garlic cloves finely chopped
1/3 cup finely chopped
  cilantro leaves
1/2 teaspoon salt

2 cups water
2 cups tomato juice
1/4 cup chopped green
  olives

Put garlic and cilantro in saucepan, sprinkle with the salt, bruise with spoon to release flavors. Add water a little at a time while stirring over medium heat. Add tomato juice and simmer 10 minutes. Serve with 1 tablespoon of the olives added to each bowl. Makes four portions.

SALAD WITH CILANTRO

This is a Chinese salad made with cilantro, which here is called Chinese parsley.

2 medium-sized, peeled kohlrabis, shredded
1 cup shredded Chinese cabbage such
  as Wong Bok
1 medium-sized carrot cut into
  matchstick pieces

1/4 cup chopped cilantro
1/4 cup salad oil
1 tablespoon vinegar
salt and pepper

Put all the vegetables in a salad bowl, pour oil and vinegar over them, season to taste with salt and pepper, toss and serve.

In China, cilantro leaves are used as a garnish for meats and seafoods, much as we use curled-leaf parsley. Chinese cooks also treat cilantro as a seasoning for barbecued chicken and duck.

⟍ COURGETTES — Europe ⟍

"Courgette" means "little squash," and these little darlings of the French are harvested when no bigger than pork sausages. Courgettes are available in several varieties, all of the zucchini-squash type, *Cucurbita pepo.* There is a white courgette and a yellow-striped green one listed by le Jardin. Thompson & Morgan carry a dark green one, and Vilmorin lists four green kinds.

Courgettes are annuals and are grown in the way described for cee gwa, but courgettes need only about two months to start producing. For this reason also, except in very short-summer climates, it is not necessary to seed courgettes indoors. Seed directly in the garden, in spots spaced 3 feet apart. They need no trellis. Plant a 12-inch circle of 6 or 8 seeds in each of the spots after working half a bushel of compost into each. Thin to the best three or four plants after they are a few inches high.

COURGETTES WITH CROUTONS

16 courgettes	salt and pepper
3 tablespoons olive oil	1 cup of 1/4-inch bread
1 garlic cloves	cubes

Cut courgettes in quarters lengthwise. Simmer them about 10 minutes in olive oil in skillet in which the garlic has been squeezed through press. Lift and turn courgettes several times with pancake turner during this cooking. When done, season with the salt and pepper and remove courgettes to a warm platter.

To the oil and juices in skillet add bread cubes, turn up heat, stir cubes until they have absorbed liquids and are lightly browned. Sprinkle them over courgettes. Makes four portions.

COURGETTES IN CREAM

16 courgettes	1/8 teaspoon ground ginger
1/4 cup water	1 tablespoon minced tarragon
2 tablespoons butter	1/3 cup cream
salt and pepper	

Cut courgettes in half lengthwise and put them in a large skillet, cut sides up. Add water, cover skillet, and simmer a few minutes until courgettes are barely fork-tender.

In separate pan melt butter, add rest of the ingredients, and simmer briefly. Drizzle this mixture over the courgettes and cook gently for 2 or 3 more minutes. Makes four portions.

COURGETTES ROQUEFORT

4 tablespoons butter	garlic clove
16 courgettes	salt and pepper
1 Welsh onion, white	1/4 cup crumbled Roquefort
part, chopped	cheese
lettuce leaves	

Melt butter in large skillet. Add courgettes and onion, cover with let-tuce, put lid on skillet and cook over medium-low heat about 15 minutes or until courgettes are barely tender. Lower heat, remove and discard lettuce, squeeze garlic clove through press into skillet, add salt, pepper, and cheese. Stir gently with rubber spatula while cheese melts and blends with vegetables. Serve at once. Makes four portions.

SCALLOPED COURGETTES

butter	1/2 teaspoon salt
12 courgettes	1/8 teaspoon pepper
1/4 cup flour	2 tablespoons minced basil
2 leeks, white parts, thinly sliced	1 cup tomato juice
	1/2 cup croutons*
1/4 teaspoon sugar	1/4 cup grated Romano cheese

Butter a casserole. Cut courgettes in half crosswise and put them in a bag with the flour, a few at a time. Hold bag shut and shake well to coat courgettes with flour. Put half the courgettes in casserole, fol-lowed by a layer of half the leeks. Repeat layers. Stir sugar, salt, pep-per and basil into the tomato juice, and pour into casserole. Spread croutons and cheese over the top. Cook uncovered in preheated 325° F. oven for 90 minutes. Makes four portions.

CREAMED COURGETTES

4 tablespoons butter	salt and pepper
16 courgettes	1 tablespoon flour
1/2 cup chopped mushrooms	1/2 cup cream
2 eschalots, finely chopped	

Melt butter in large skillet. Add courgettes and cook over brisk heat, stirring, for 3 minutes. Reduce heat, cover skillet, cook for about 5 more minutes. Add mushrooms and eschalots, cook covered for another 5 minutes. Season with salt and pepper and remove with slotted turner to serving dish. Keep warm.

Stir flour into cream until well-blended, then slowly stir it into juices in skillet until smooth. Cook over low heat, stirring, until slightly thickened. Do not let it come to a boil. Pour over courgettes and serve at once. Makes four portions.

OVEN COURGETTES

12 courgettes	2 tablespoons butter
2 fresh ripe tomatoes	1/2 cup coarse fresh bread
1/4 teaspoon dried dill	crumbs
1/2 teaspoon salt	Port d'Salut cheese
1/4 teaspoon pepper	

Parboil courgettes in water or vegetable stock until fork-tender. Drain. Put them into a shallow baking dish. Slightly crush tomatoes and place them on the courgettes. Sprinkle with the seasonings. Melt butter in skillet, stir bread crumbs into it and cook, stirring, until crumbs are lightly browned. Spread them over vegetables in baking dish. Lay strips of the cheese over the crumb topping in lattice pattern. Bake uncovered at 400° F. about 20 minutes. Makes two portions.

⌁ DAIKON – Orient ⌁

"Daikon" is Japanese for radish, and these radishes are different from the ones we know. However, they are the same species as ours—*Raphanus sativus* var. *longipinnatus*—and are biennials grown as annuals.

It is hard for most Americans to realize how importantly the radish looms as a food in the Orient. Instead of being an incidental little relish and salad vegetable, the Oriental radish is said to be the most widely eaten vegetable in Japan.

In most cases the daikon is much larger than our radish and takes longer to mature, although they may be eaten at any stage of growth. The daikon greatly lengthens the radish season and needs only ordinary radish culture. Spade soil deeply, working in compost. Thin daikon plants 6 to 12 inches apart, according to the size of roots at maturity. Most roots range up to 2 feet long, with weights reaching up to four or five pounds.

For spring seeding a good variety is Tokinashi; the 18-inch white root is crisp and hot and matures in about two months. For early summer seeding, good ones are Osaka Shijunichi, Minowase, and Akahime, each maturing in six weeks or so. The winter daikon is seeded in July and August for a late fall and winter harvest and can be dug and stored in the cellar like a turnip. Some winter varieties are the mild Myashige and the Ohkura, which grow tapered roots, and

Daikon, or Japanese radish, grows a large root that remains crisp over the long growing and storage period. W. ATLEE BURPEE CO.

two round-rooted ones: Shogoin, which grows to grapefruit size, and Sakurajima, which can grow to the size of a basketball or larger and can weigh fifty pounds or more if it has five frost-free months in which to grow.

Daikon selections are offered by Grace, Gurney, Hudson, Johnny, Kitazawa, Nichols, and Redwood.

As an addition—a garnish—to soups, the daikon is sliced thinly in 2-inch-long matchsticks and simmered a few minutes until tender.

A tasty appetizer is made by grating a daikon and mixing with lemon juice and salt to taste—about ½ cup grated daikon to 1 teaspoon lemon juice. Eat it as a relish or use it as a dip for strips of other vegetables. Thin slices of daikon are also marinated in vinegar.

DAIKON SALAD

1-1/2 cups shredded daikon
1 small carrot, shredded
1 tablespoon vinegar
1 teaspoon sugar
1/8 teaspoon salt

Combine daikon and carrot in bowl. Sprinkle with the other ingredients, stir lightly, and serve.

To add flavor to a mild daikon, dried hot peppers are pressed between halves of daikon or inserted in holes in the sides, something like larding a piece of meat. The daikon picks up the pepper flavor in a few hours. Remove and discard pepper before serving daikon.

Doan gwa is the Chinese name for this melon, also called Chinese winter melon, and famous as the essential ingredient in the Chinese winter melon soup. TSANG & MA INTERNATIONAL

Slices of daikon are prepared by salting them and weighting them down overnight or longer to press out some of their juice. You can also pickle a daikon as you would pickle a cucumber, using vinegar and flavorings. In China and Japan the daikon is brined.

For an attractive side dish with roast beef, cut a daikon in slices ½-inch thick, dip them in lightly beaten egg, then in fine dry bread crumbs, and cook them in oil in a skillet until light brown.

～ DOAN GWA – Orient ～

This Oriental delicacy is a melon, known as the Chinese winter melon or the wax gourd. It looks a good deal like a medium-small watermelon, stores as well as a winter squash, and is an annual, botanically *Benincasa hispida,* of the melon family. It has been enjoyed in China for many centuries.

To grow doan gwa you will need rich soil and a long warm growing season, about five months, although you can get a head start with indoor seeding in peat pots about six weeks before mild weather is expected.

As with other vining plants, you can grow doan gwa in a "hill" or spot planting. Dig a bushel-sized hole in an all-day sunny spot. Fill it two-thirds full of compost mixed with ½ pound of cottonseed meal, and finish filling with fertile soil. Plant 8 seeds 1½ inches deep in an 8-inch circle in the center of this spot, and thin to 3 plants after they are 3 inches tall. Or set out 3 indoor-grown plants in the spot, spacing them 8 inches apart.

Deep watering once a week or more frequently after fruits start growing is good practice. A 6-inch mulch of compost after plants are growing strongly is also a good idea.

Harvest the melons by cutting the stems with pruning shears, leaving a 2-inch stub attached to the fruit. Handle carefully and store in a cool, dry place. Fruits can grow up to fifteen to twenty-five pounds each and have a name for storing well for as long as a year.

Tsang & Ma list doan gwa.

Doan gwa has sweetish white flesh, looking somewhat like that of the honey dew melon, but doan gwa is not eaten raw. It is best known as the essential ingredient of the Chinese winter-melon soup.

WINTER-MELON SOUP

Cut off the stem end of a doan gwa, remove seeds, and reserve the cut-off end for a lid. Fill the doan gwa with chicken broth and with an assortment of such other ingredients as small chunks of raw chicken or pork, mushrooms, bamboo shoots, and water chestnuts.

Replace the lid, and steam the doan gwa for several hours. When the soup is ladled from the melon, pieces of melon flesh are scooped out with it.

For a simpler version, peel the doan gwa and simmer chunks of the flesh in a fish or chicken stock for 15 minutes. Any of the other ingredients above can be included.

When used in other ways, doan gwa flesh is usually steamed tender or simmered in a vegetable or meat stock. It can then be combined with a meat—pork or chicken are the most popular—and served without further ado. Other cooks prefer to thicken the dish with Chinese gravy.* An interesting addition is slivered almonds or dry-roasted peanuts.

⟿ DOW GAUK – Orient ⟿

Dow gauk is the Chinese name for a bean that grows to a length of 18 to 36 inches. An annual, it is occasionally seen in U.S. seed catalogs, sometimes listed as yard-long bean or asparagus bean. It doesn't taste like asparagus or quite like other beans. The glossy, pencil-round pods are sweet and rather crisp. The botanical name is *Vigna sesquipedalis*, and it is related to the black-eyed pea.

Give dow gauk a trellis to climb in a sunny spot. Seed it after the weather is warm, digging a 2-inch layer of compost into the site

Dow gauk is a bean, sometimes called yard-long bean, for the good reason that the crisp sweet pods actually can grow a yard long. The plant wants a warm summer. TSANG & MA INTERNATIONAL

first. Thin plants to 6 inches apart and give them a side-dressing of cottonseed meal, a pound to 25 feet of row, when they begin to flower. The vines grow to 6 or 8 feet high.

The harvest begins in about eleven weeks—with some luck, since the plant is a temperamental tropical and won't grow if conditions do not please it. It does best in the South.

Houses listing dow gauk are Burgess, Hudson, Field, Grace, Gurney, Kitazawa, and Tsang & Ma.

Like snow peas, these beans should be harvested young, when the seeds are just starting to show on the sides of the pods.

Chinese like this bean combined with beef, pork, or shrimps in a stir-fry. This cooking method retains the bean's crispness. The pods are cut into 3-inch pieces, cooked in oil with a piece of garlic for 5 minutes. They are then served with cooked shrimp, strips of cooked beef, or strips of cooked pork mixed in.

Another way to serve the beans is to stir-fry them in oil 5 minutes, then serve them dressed with a mixture of soy sauce and crushed toasted sesame seeds.*

DOW GAUK AND BEEF

1/2 pound of beef chopped
  medium-fine
2-3 tablespoons oil
2 cups dow gauk cut in
  1/4-inch pieces
2 green onions cut in
  1/4-inch pieces

1/4 cup chopped water
  chestnuts
1 cup chopped mushrooms
1 teaspoon minced Chinese
  chives
1/2 cup Cathay sauce*

In wok or heavy iron skillet stir-fry beef in oil over high heat 2-3 minutes. Add dow gauk and stir-fry 3-4 more minutes. Add onions, water chestnuts, and mushrooms, and stir-fry 2-3 more minutes. Remove from fire, stir in Chinese chives, serve dressed with Cathay sauce.

Young leaves and stems of dow gauk are also eaten in China, steamed and served with oil or butter.

⌒ ESCHALOTS – Europe ⌒

Onions are among the world's most cosmopolitan vegetables, and the most patrician branch of the family is the eschalot, *Allium ascalonicum.* An eschalot, or shallot, is about the size of a garlic clove and is enclosed in a papery brownish or gray sheath. It grows just below ground level or just a bit above it at the tip, in a loosely connected bunch of about a dozen.

Most eschalots are imported, but they have been grown for years in Louisiana for the New Orleans market. There you also find fresh eschalots, looking like spring onions, but it is the mature dried bulbs that the great majority of eschalot fanciers know. (However, eschalots are perennials, like chives, and can be left in the garden to be harvested green, as needed. In cold climates they will need a winter mulch.)

To grow eschalots, plant them in early spring in a fertile spot where they won't get watered quite as much as the other vegetables. The larger the bulbs you plant, the better and more productive the plants will grow. Set the bulbs with pointed ends up, the tips just below ground level. Space them 6 inches apart. They make their leaf growth in cool weather and follow with bulb growth in summer. They take about four months to mature, and this is signaled by their tops turning brown. Dig the bulbs at this time, dry them outdoors for a few days, then store them in a dry place, preferably an airy one, at room temperature.

Eschalots are being listed by more seedsmen than handled them a few years ago. Sources are Burpee, Farmer, Johnny, le Jardin, Metro Myster, and Thompson & Morgan. Some eschalot seed is offered also, but bulbs are more dependable.

The role of eschalots in cooking is almost entirely that of a flavoring, and they are among the great ones. Fairly strong raw, they become subtle and delightful when cooked. Like garlic, they are prepared for use by stripping off the papery covering and are often chopped finely to distribute their flavor well. Also like garlic, they

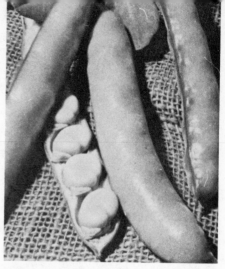

The ancient fava bean is well-known in Europe and grows in cool weather. Its flattish green beans taste something like peas. J. A. DEMONCHAUX CO.

burn easily, so avoid high heat when sauteeing or braising eschalots, or add them late in the cooking period.

Eschalots are an essential ingredient in duxelles (see chapter three).

FAVA BEANS — Europe, Orient

Fava beans are one of the most ancient of cultivated vegetables. They are also known as broad beans, windsor beans, giant English beans, European beans, etc. In France they are *feve,* in Spain, *haba.* Their flavor is pea-like, and they are also a cool-weather annual, as are peas. Consequently, favas, which are botanically *Vicia faba* and relatives of vetch, are seeded in early spring for a crop three to four months later or in the fall in mild areas for a spring crop.

Favas need plenty of moisture but are not otherwise demanding if the climate suits them. They grow 3 feet high, sometimes higher, and need only simple support, such as a wire or twine line stretched along each side of the row.

The circular, shiny green, flattened beans grow in pods 8 to 12 inches long or longer, borne on the stalk. Favas are listed by Burpee, de Giorgi, Demonchaux, Johnny, le Jardin, Nichols, Redwood, Suttons, and Thompson & Morgan.

Fava beans are popular in Europe, but few Americans have tasted them. They are usually shelled like lima beans before or after being cooked tender in water. At this point, young fava beans can be finished with a simmering in butter. Older favas need to have the outer coat removed first. This is done by squeezing the bean or by peeling it off.

It is a fact that some people cannot eat fava beans, due to an allergic reaction. Sample with caution if you don't know whether favas agree with you.

FAVA BEAN POT

This dish is popular with the Portuguese.

3 cups shelled fava beans
4 green onions cut in
  1/4-inch pieces
1 tablespoon chopped parsley
1 tablespoon chopped marjoram
2 garlic cloves, minced

1/4 cup olive oil
1/4 cup vegetable oil
1 tablespoon red wine
  vinegar
1/2 teaspoon cayenne sauce
salt and pepper

Simmer beans in water until fork-tender. Drain and cool. Peel beans and add the rest of the ingredients to them in a saucepan. Simmer covered for an hour. Makes four portions. Can be stored in the refrigerator and reheated.

FAVAS AND MUSHROOMS

2 cups shelled fava beans
2 leeks, chopped
6-8 large mushrooms sliced
  thinly

1 tablespoon chopped parsley
1 garlic clove, minced
1/4 cup olive oil
salt and pepper

Cook beans fork-tender in water. Drain and peel. Put them in saucepan and add the other ingredients. Cover pan and cook over medium heat about 8 minutes, shaking pan frequently. Makes four portions.

⟶ FENUGREEK — Africa, Europe, Orient ⟿

Fenugreek is botanically *Trigonella foenum-graecum,* a hardy annual legume that looks a good deal like clover. It grows erect to about 2 feet.

Seed fenugreek in the spring after weather is mild, and thin plants 3 or 4 inches apart. They will do best in a sunny spot.

Fenugreek's aromatic leaves can be cooked like spinach, but the seeds are the important food part of the plant. These seeds are carried in sickle-shaped pods. Let them mature on the plants, then shell them out for use dry.

Fenugreek seed is listed by Hudson, Johnny, Metro Myster, Redwood, and Thompson & Morgan.

Fenugreek's brown seeds smell something like caramelized sugar or maple syrup and taste mildly bitter. They are crushed for use as a flavoring, usually for the kind of foods that ground cloves or nutmeg might go into, and fenugreek can be substituted for these spices.

Another interesting use for fenugreek seeds is as a coffee alternative. Roast the seeds at 250° F. for 30 minutes or until thoroughly dried. Then crush or grind them and proceed as with ground coffee. Or stir 1 tablespoon of the ground seeds into 1 cup of boiling water, let it steep for 5 minutes covered, then strain.

Still another way of using this versatile seed is to sprout them like mung beans. Fenugreek sprouts are sweet and spicy and highly nutritious. If you don't have a commercial sprouter, put 2 or 3 tablespoons of fenugreek seeds and 1 cup of water in a quart canning jar, let stand about 10 minutes, then drain off the water. Cover the jar with cheesecloth and put it in a warm place. Rinse and drain 2 or 3 times a day until sprouts are big enough to use. Try them braised in a little olive oil with thinly sliced and parboiled cardoon stalks.

In the Near East the sprouts are put into a lamb stew traditionally flavored with honey.

⟿ FETTICUS – Europe ⟿

Fetticus recommends itself to the gardener as an undemanding, mild-flavored leafy green that will give a generous harvest. The spoon-shaped leaves, formed in dense rosettes, are a popular salad green in France. Fetticus is an annual, *Valerianella locusta* var. *olitoria*, and is also called vetticost, lamb's lettuce, mache, and corn salad.

Seed it in early spring (March in the Midwest) for harvesting in May or in late summer for a fall harvest, which will extend into winter if plants are protected with a strawy mulch. Seeding can be close— ¼ inch between seeds—and the thinnings can be used in salads when surplus plants are removed to give the others 6-inch spading. Do this

Fetticus is called maché in France, where the spoon-shaped leaves are enjoyed in salads. J. A. DEMONCHAUX CO.

thinning two or three weeks after seeding. Plants mature in about two months and can be harvested a leaf at a time, if desired, for weeks afterward.

Several U.S. seed houses list fetticus, usually as corn salad. Vilmorin lists six varieties, three of which are carried by le Jardin.

In France, Roquefort cheese is particularly liked with fetticus in a salad. Crumble the cheese and sprinkle it over the dressed and tossed salad.

FETTICUS WITH TOMATOES

The bland flavor of fetticus combines well with the other ingredients of this Italian dish.

2 green onions cut in 1/4-inch
    pieces
1 tablespoon butter
1 tablespoon olive oil
3 cups rinsed and coarsely
    chopped fetticus

6 Italian tomatoes cut in
    1/2-inch slices
1 tablespoon garlic vinegar
salt and pepper

In a skillet cook onions in butter and oil over medium-low heat for a few minutes. Stir in fetticus, lower heat, cover pan, cook 10 minutes. Add remaining ingredients, increase heat and cook, stirring, for 2-3 minutes. The tomatoes are to be warmed through but not quite cooked. Serve at once. Makes four portions.

Their shape will tell you why these little northern European delicacies are called fingerling potatoes. They are indeed plumply finger-shaped or thumb-shaped, a few inches long and an inch or more in diameter, with yellowish flesh of a distinctive, slightly sweet flavor.

Early German settlers introduced fingerlings in the Upper Midwest. One seldom sees them being grown elsewhere, and the only gardener we found raising them had obtained tubers from Europe through a foreign-born friend. However, there are the two domestic suppliers, Gurney and Olds.

Culture is the same as for white potatoes. Plant fingerling tubers whole, 2-3 inches deep, in early spring in well-spaded, compost-enriched soil in a sunny, non-soggy spot. Space plantings 12 inches apart. When plants are growing well, work 2 tablespoons of cottonseed meal into the soil around each one. Dig the crop when the tops die, which will be in approximately 3 months. Store in a dark place. Fingerlings are known for good production.

GERMAN POTATO SALAD

This recipe is said to be like one made famous by an old St. Louis restaurant, Speck's.

3 pounds fingerling potatoes	4 teaspoons sugar
2 strips lean bacon	2/3 cup cider vinegar
1 whole green onion, chopped	1/3 cup water
1 tablespoon flour	1/2 teaspoon celery seed
2 teaspoons salt	3 tablespoons chopped parsley
1/4 teaspoon pepper	2 egg whites, lightly beaten

Steam unpeeled potatoes until fork-tender. While they are cooking, proceed with the next steps:

Fry bacon crisp, remove from pan, and cut with kitchen shears into ¼-inch squares. Put bacon in warm place and cook onion in drippings for 1 minute. Stir in the flour, salt, pepper, and sugar. Blend in vinegar and water, simmer 10 minutes, stirring. Cover to keep warm while you quickly peel potatoes, which should be hot, slice them as thick as half-dollars, put them in a bowl and pour over them the contents of skillet, the reserved bacon squares, celery seed, parsley, and egg whites. Toss gently and serve warm. Makes six portions.

FINGERLING POTATOES AU GRATIN

1-1/2 pounds fingerling potatoes
3 tablespoons butter
2 eschalots, minced
2 tablespoons flour
1 cup milk

1/2 teaspoon salt
1/8 teaspoon pepper
1/8 teaspoon grated nutmeg
1/4 cup grated Parmesan
  cheese

Steam potatoes tender. While they are cooking, melt butter in a saucepan, add eschalots, and simmer over low heat 2 minutes. Stir in flour, simmer another minute. Add milk, stir until liquid thickens. Season with salt, pepper, and nutmeg. Peel potatoes, cut into ¼-inch slices, add to other ingredients in saucepan. Stir gently, pour into buttered baking dish, sprinkle with cheese. Bake at 350° F. until golden brown on top. Makes four portions.

BREAKFAST POTATOES

4-6 fingerling potatoes
2 tablespoons butter

2 teaspoons olive oil
salt

Peel potatoes, cut into quarters lengthwise, cut quarters into nickel-thick slices. Melt butter in skillet, add oil, stir in potatoes, covering bottom of skillet evenly. Cover and cook over medium-low heat 7 minutes, stirring a few times. Uncover skillet, salt potatoes lightly, turn them upside down, and cook 3 more minutes. Serve at once. Makes two portions.

SKILLET FINGERLING POTATOES

2 tablespoons butter
4-6 fingerling potatoes, peeled
salt and pepper
white parts of two green onions
  finely chopped

1 tablespoon finely
  chopped chervil
1/2 cup rich milk

Melt butter in skillet. Using potato peeler, thinly slice potatoes directly into skillet, covering bottom evenly. Cook over medium heat 2-3 minutes. Season with salt and pepper. Sprinkle onions and chervil over potatoes. Carefully pour milk into skillet and simmer 5-10 minutes longer, or until milk is absorbed. Fold potatoes into a half-circle and cut into two pie-slices. Serve at once. Makes two portions.

Like kohlrabi, finnochio grows an edible kind of bulb just above ground level. And like kohlrabi, finnochio is a stranger to most American home gardens—which is too bad, for it is a fine vegetable. An annual, it is also called Florence fennel, and botanically, it is *Foeniculum vulgare* var. *dulce.* It is a willing grower that likes a sunny spot in fertile soil.

Seed directly in the garden in late spring in rows about 2 feet apart, and thin plants 6-8 inches apart in the rows. Give them a compost mulch when they are 8-10 inches tall. They grow to 2 feet or more and are lovely ferny-leaved plants. Bulbs mature in three months and can be harvested younger.

Several seed houses list finnochio, usually as fennel or Florence fennel, sometimes among herbs. Strictly speaking, the herbal fennel is called sweet fennel, but it and finnochio are closely related. If you let a finnochio plant go to seed, you can use the seed as a flavoring agent. Finnochio's leaves can also be used for flavoring.

Years ago, finnochio seeds were eaten like candy, usually after being given a sugar coating.

Finnochio's rather tarragonlike taste does not appeal to everyone, but we urge you to give it a chance to win you over. The bulb is prepared for cooking by trimming away the top stalks and outer sheath of stalk bases.

FINNOCHIO SALAD 1

Finnochio is eaten raw, like celery, in this Italian salad.

1 finnochio bulb	1 tablespoon lemon juice
2 green onions	1/2 cup commercial sour
1/8 teaspoon salt	cream

Remove stalky top of finnochio bulb. Slice bulb lengthwise into eighths. Chop green onions coarsely, put them and finnochio into salad bowl, sprinkle with the salt. Mix lemon juice and sour cream, blend gently with finnochio and onions. Makes four portions.

FINNOCHIO SALAD 2

1 finnochio bulb	1/4 cup finely chopped chives
1 cup French dressing*	1/4 cup broken cashew nuts

Trim finnochio bulb, cut into eighths lengthwise, cook barely tender in a little water. Drain, marinate segments in the dressing for 30 minutes in salad bowl. Then add chives, stir lightly, and serve sprinkled with the cashew pieces. Makes four portions.

FINNOCHIO IN THE GREEK MANNER

This recipe is a basic one that you can adapt to a number of other vegetables. The general rule for choosing which to use is that they should be non-dominant in flavor. Vegetables cooked in this way are particularly good for garnishing a salad plate.

2 medium-sized finnochio bulbs	sprig of spearmint
1/4 cup wine vinegar	sprig of lemon thyme
1/4 cup olive oil	half a bay leaf
1/8 teaspoon celery seed	salt

Trim and quarter finnochio bulbs. Put them in saucepan with water to half cover them. Add remaining ingredients except salt. Cover pan, simmer until finnochio is fork-tender. Drain and chill. Salt lightly before serving. Makes four portions.
The cooking liquid can be kept for future similar use.

～ FLAGEOLETS – Europe ～

Flageolets are a type of haricot (French bean) related to and resembling our snap beans, but the flageolet is a small-seeded bush shell bean, usually shelled out like lima beans. Also like limas, flageolets are eaten both fresh and dried. They are called haricots flageolets when used as fresh shell beans and haricots secs when dried. Fanciers of flageolets swear that nothing can take their place in such dishes as the famous cassoulet, despairing whenever navy beans are suggested as a substitute.

Botanically *Phaseolus vulgaris*, flageolets are annuals. You grow them as you do snap beans (see adzuki beans), seeding after weather is mild, in full sun and in compost-enriched soil. The harvest is not as heavy as from snap beans, so successive plantings at two-week intervals is a good plan if you have the garden space. Demonchaux and Suttons list the excellent Chevrier flageolet; le Jardin lists two other good kinds; and Vilmorin lists eight.

To get dried flageolets, let the pods dry on the plants, then finish the drying by cutting plants at ground level and hanging them in an airy place. When pods are dry enough so beans can easily be shelled out, do so. Then put them in shallow pans and place them in the oven at 140° F. for an hour. Store in capped jars at room temperature.

FRENCH BEAN SALAD

1 cup dried flageolets	1 head curled endive, chopped
1 tablespoon oil	2 tablespoons minced chervil
1/2 cup French dressing*	

Soak beans overnight in 1 quart of water. Next morning transfer them to saucepan, adding more water to cover them if necessary. Add the oil. Cook beans until barely tender, about an hour. The beans should absorb all the water during this cooking.

Put warm beans in bowl and immediately pour the dressing over them. Let them rest for 2 hours or longer at room temperature. Serve them on the endive, and sprinkle beans with the chervil. Makes four portions.

We sometimes add to this salad matchstick strips of ham or broiled bacon. Served with breadsticks, this makes a complete luncheon dish.

CASSOULET

There is a great deal of leeway among cassoulet recipes, but basically a cassoulet is a bean and meat dish. The recipe we give here is our gradual adaptation of parts from several others, and it is our favorite.

2 cups dried flageolets	lard or butter, if needed
1 onion, sliced	2 garlic cloves, minced
2 teaspoons salt	2 tomatoes, chopped
1/4 teaspoon pepper	2 tablespoons minced
2 cups vegetable stock	parsley
1/2 pound smoked garlic sausage	1 teaspoon minced thyme
4 small white onions, peeled	2 tablespoons extract of
1 pound lamb shoulder cut into	goose meat (optional)
1/2-inch cubes	1 cup beef stock
1 pound fresh pork shoulder	
cut into 1/2-inch cubes	

Soak flageolets in 2 quarts of water overnight. Next morning drain off any water remaining, put beans in large pot, and add the sliced onion, salt, pepper, and vegetable stock. Bring to a boil and simmer, covered, for an hour.

In a large skillet, fry sausage until well-browned. Remove, cut into ½-inch chunks, and add to the beans.

In the fat from sausage in the skillet, brown the onions and add them to the beans.

Sear the lamb and pork meat in the skillet, adding lard or butter if there is not enough sausage fat left. Cover skillet and simmer lamb and pork 30 minutes.

Finally, add the lamb, pork, and the remaining ingredients to the beans. Simmer for 2 hours or transfer to a large casserole and bake for 2 hours at 350° F. Add more liquid if needed; the consistency should be about that of baked beans. Check seasoning before serving. Makes about 3 quarts.

Any leftover portion can be frozen or stored in the refrigerator for reheating a few days later. When reheating, add ½ cup of any stock or water.

Flageolets are very good served with bechamel sauce.* Dried flageolets are favored; soak in water overnight, cook them tender, heap them into a warm bowl, and pour the sauce over them. Chop a few sprigs of cress or parsley over the dish just before serving.

FLAGEOLET CASSEROLE

3 cups fresh flageolets	1 garlic clove
2 medium-large tomatoes	1/2 teaspoon salt
2 tablespoons minced parsley	butter
1 tablespoon minced savory	1 cup croutons*

Cook flageolets in water until tender. Drain. Peel and chop tomatoes and add to flageolets. Stir in parsley, savory, garlic squeezed through press, and salt. Butter a casserole, put mixture into it, sprinkle croutons on top. Bake uncovered for 30 minutes at 300° F. Makes four portions.

We offer the following two recipes through the courtesy of seedsman J.A. Demonchaux.

FRESH GREEN FLAGEOLET BEANS

After shelling the beans, pour them in salted boiling water. *Add bouquet garni* and simmer for about one hour.* Do not cover *so that they will remain green.*

Drain beans. Sauté in butter and add finely cut parsley. Delicious with lamb.

DRIED GREEN FLAGEOLET BEANS

We usually soak them overnight. Pour dried flageolet beans in unsalted cold water *and bring them to a rapid boil. Add bouquet garni,** cover, *and simmer for 2 hours.*

Season with salt and proceed as above.

⌐ FOO GWA – Orient ⌐

Foo gwa, also called the Chinese bitter melon, or bitter gourd, is botanically *Momordica charantia,* a variety of balsam pear, and is an annual. Foo gwa fruits are warty-skinned little fellows, pointed at the tips and growing to 8 inches long but harvested younger. The plant is a handsome climber.

Foo gwa needs about ten weeks of warm weather. Seed it in late spring, along a fence or trellis 5-6 feet high. Space plants 6 inches apart. Before seeding, work a 6-inch layer of compost into the row along with 1 pound of cottonseed meal to 10 feet of row. Foo gwa seeds are slow to germinate, so water the soil well just before seeding, plant seeds 1 inch deep, cover with soil and then with black plastic as described for Chinese celery.

Foo gwa is listed by Grace, Kitazawa, and Tsang & Ma.

Foo gwa's light green flesh has a bitter tang. Harvest the fruits at 4-6 inches long, while they are green and young. To prepare the melon for cooking, cut it in half lengthwise, and with a spoon scrape out seeds and fiber. A brief parboiling, or a steeping in salt water, will reduce the bitterness, if wished, before using the melon in any of the following ways. Peeling is not necessary.

Chunks or balls of foo gwa are dropped into simmering chicken or beef broth for 5 minutes to make an Eastern soup.

A simple stir-fry is made by cooking diced foo gwa with chopped cooked chicken in oil. Chopped tops of green onions are sometimes added during the last few seconds.

A basic flavoring for foo gwa, used in the next two recipes, is made like this:

FOO GWA SAUCE

3 teaspoons cured black soy bean (dow sei)	1 teaspoon sugar
	2 teaspoons soy sauce
2 cloves garlic	2 teaspoons oil

Rinse the dow sei well (it can be bought in Chinese markets), chop garlic, and mash with dow sei in a mortar or bowl. Work in the sugar, soy sauce, and oil, in that order, until a smooth paste is formed. If not needed at once, store covered in refrigerator.

For stir-frying, heat 2 tablespoons of oil in a wok or heavy skillet, add 1 tablespoon of foo gwa sauce, and cook, stirring, for 2 minutes. Add 2 cups diced foo gwa, and stir-fry until fork-tender.

STUFFED FOO GWA

4 halves foo gwa, cleaned and parboiled	1/2 cup cooked shrimps, chopped
1/2 pound ground pork, lightly fried	1 recipe foo gwa sauce*

Fill foo gwa halves with the other ingredients well-mixed together. Bake 40 minutes in preheated 350° F. oven. Makes four portions.

"Strawberries of the woods," the fraises des bois of Europe, are botanically *Fragaria vesca*. Perennials, they include the perpetual strawberries and the Alpines, and are basically wildlings that adapt beautifully to garden culture. The plants are delicate looking little things, standing 8 or 9 inches tall, bearing smaller and lighter green leaves than other strawberries. Their tapered little berries are perhaps a quarter the size of an ordinary medium-sized strawberry.

It is the piquant wildish taste of these little berries, however, that has won the hearts of epicures over the centuries. We grew them as a garden path edging, in a West seacoast location that was not kind to strawberries, hurting the fruit quality of all the varieties we raised. We liked the fraises des bois for their easy adaptability, though, and neat growth. We were growing an Alpine type. Incidentally, the attractive little berries delight children, and the plants are one of those we recommend for children to grow.

Instead of setting out plants, you grow fraises des bois from seed. You can sow it directly in the garden (indeed, our Alpines did their own such seeding, and the resulting volunteers were excellent plants). But it is safer to begin by starting the seed in flats, as they take about a month to germinate. Give seedlings another six weeks to grow before moving them to the garden.

Choose an open location with compost generously dug in beforehand. If you get the plants to the garden by April, you should have fruit that fall. After the first year, the plants bear fruit from spring through late fall. They seem to need little fertilizing. We gave it to them in the form of compost mulch.

Fraises des bois do not form runners, but individual plants grow larger and can be divided like clumps of chives into three or four plants in early spring.

Among seed houses listing Alpine or related kinds of these strawberries are Burpee, de Giorgi, Demonchaux, Gurney, Hudson, Johnny, le Jardin, Park, Thompson & Morgan, and Vilmorin.

These elfin berries are so tempting in the garden, it is sometimes difficult to get enough for serving. But they are so exquisite that just a few make an epicurean dessert. The way we like to serve them is with Devonshire cream, this being possible at times when we have our own cow.

DEVONSHIRE CREAM

Put fresh-from-the-cow milk in a large pan and cover with a cloth. Let is stand in a cool basement 24 hours. Next, put the pan on the lowest possible heat on the range, and bring milk just to scalding (when pinpoint holes begin showing on the surface) but never let it boil. Immediately remove pan from heat, set it carefully in a cool place, let stand 6-12 hours. Then skim the cream—the thick, smooth, delicious Devonshire cream.

When we don't have a cow, we make a kind of Devonshire cream using either of the following recipes:

SOUR CREAM "DEVONSHIRE"

Put 1 cup of commercial sour cream in a small bowl, and stir in 1 teaspoon of fresh lemon juice. If the consistency is too stiff, add 1 tablespoon or less of cream.

CREAM CHEESE "DEVONSHIRE"

Put contents of an 8-ounce package of cream cheese in a small bowl. Work in 1 teaspoon fresh lemon juice. If needed, add enough cream to let you form a soft mound.

Using either genuine Devonshire cream or one of the other two, we place a mound of the cream on a small dessert plate and surround it with the little berries still wearing their jaunty caps. We serve a bowl of powdered sugar also, but most people prefer just to dip the berries in the cream without sugar.

For best results, pick the berries no more than an hour or two before serving. Rinse them quickly after picking, place them on paper towels on a tray, and put them in a cool place (not the refrigerator). Serve at room temperature.

CHOCOLATE-COATED FRAISES DES BOIS

Here is a way to make the berries go a little further.

Pick and rinse berries and put on paper towels in a cool, airy place until completely dry—very dry.

Next, melt in the top of a double boiler enough sweet chocolate to coat the berries. Let melted chocolate cool to room temperature.

Then, holding the berries by their stems, dip each into the chocolate, coating most of the berry except the cap and stem. Lay them carefully on waxed paper on a cooky sheet and put them in the refrigerator for an hour or two before serving.

For a charming and nutritious dessert, turn cup custards out of molds onto individual dessert plates, top them with a dollop of freshly whipped cream, and decorate with a chocolate-covered strawberry.

✦ FRENCH CARROTS — Europe ✦

The French make a culinary specialty of the carrot and have developed some excellent varieties. Most of them look like the carrots familiar to all of us—cone-shaped and more or less tapering—but another, and one we urge you to try, is nearly round, from ping pong to golf ball size according to variety, and a delicious, sweet little morsel. De Giorgi carries a variety called Parisian, Grace lists Parisian Ball, Suttons carry the two-inch wide Parisian Ronda, and Thompson & Morgan list Konfrix. All are fast growers. Carrots are biennials grown as annuals. Botanically, they are *Daucus carota sativa*.

It is standard practice to spade soil deeply for carrots, and while we don't discourage doing so for these little round French ones, they don't insist on it. Compost dug in at seeding time is welcome, however, and so is a pound of cottonseed meal to 25 feet of row. Thin the young plants to stand about 1 inch apart. Two months is normal maturity time, and carrots can be left in the ground for a good while, to be used as needed.

If you have trouble getting carrots to germinate, follow directions given for Chinese celery on covering the seed bed with sheet plastic.

CARROT CASSEROLE

12 boiling onions, peeled	1/2 teaspoon salt
12 round French carrots, scrubbed and parboiled 5 minutes	1/8 teaspoon pepper
	1/2 cup butter
	1 garlic clove
2 cups of 1/2-inch potato balls	1 teaspoon lemon juice
1/4 teaspoon ground cloves	1 teaspoon honey

Put onions, carrots, and potato balls in casserole. Sprinkle with cloves, salt, and pepper. Stir gently to blend.

In a saucepan melt the butter, squeeze garlic clove into it through press, stir in lemon juice and honey. Pour the mixture over the vegetables in casserole, distributing it evenly. Cover casserole and bake for 60 minutes at 325° F. Makes four portions.

GLAZED CARROTS

1/4 cup butter
20 round French carrots,
  scrubbed and parboiled
5 minutes

1/4 cup cream sherry
dash of Angostura bitters
salt

Melt butter in saucepan, add carrots, turn up heat, and cook, shaking pan frequently, until carrots are lightly browned. Reduce heat to low, add sherry, bitters, and salt to taste. Stir to blend. Cover pan and simmer 10-15 minutes with occasional stirring. Most of the wine will be absorbed by the carrots, and juices remaining in pan should be poured over the carrots when they are put into serving bowl. Makes four portions.

GAI LOHN – Orient

This fast-growing plant, gai lohn, is a member of the cabbage group, its botanical name being *Brassica alboglabra*. It is grown as an annual. Commonly called Chinese kale or Chinese broccoli, it grows edible flower buds like broccoli, although they are less prominent. The plant's ultimate height is 12-14 inches.

Like its relatives, gai lohn is a cool-weather lover, seeded in early March for a May-June harvest and in August for an October-November one. Grow it as you do Chinese cabbage, but space gai lohn plants only 6 inches apart.

The large leaves and the stems as well as the flower buds of gai lohn are eaten. Gather the buds before they open, taking the central stem bud first in order to force development of side shoots.

Grace and Tsang & Ma list gai lohn, and Redwood carries it as Chinese broccoli.

Gai lohn can be cooked like broccoli, for which it is an acceptable substitute.

In the Orient, gai lohn is frequently stir-fried. The stalks are cut into 2-inch lengths for this purpose.

Gai lohn is steamed or simmered in water until barely tender, then served with oyster sauce, which is available in Oriental and some other food markets.

GAI LOHN AND PORK

1/2 pound fresh pork
2-3 tablespoons garlic-flavored oil
3 cups of gai lohn cut into 1-inch pieces

1 tablespoon minced cilantro (Chinese parsley)
salt

Cut pork into thin strips 2 inches long and stir-fry 5-6 minutes in the oil, in heavy skillet. Add gai lohn and stir-fry 3-4 minutes. Season with cilantro and salt during the last few seconds of cooking and serve at once. Makes four portions.

GOBO – Orient

If you called gobo a weed, you would be almost right. It is related to burdock, *Arctium minus,* which certainly is a weed, but *A. lappa,* which is often lumped in with its weed cousin, is cultivated in Japan as a root vegetable. Other names for gobo are edible burdock and edible goberon. It gets to be quite a plant, up to 8 feet tall, with big leaves shaped like Valentine hearts, green on top and light gray-green underneath. Culture is much as for carrots—deep spading (extra-deep for gobo), before seed is sown, in late spring for a late fall harvest.

Gobo is weed enough to grow with little attention and in almost any site, although preferably in a neutral, pH 7.0, soil. Its purplish flowers produce burrs in which the seeds are contained, so keep flowers pinched off to prevent self-seeding, which could become a weed problem.

Johnny lists two varieties of gobo, Watambe Early, which grows a 30-inch root and is recommended for heavy soils, and the more commonly seen Takinogawa, whose root can grow to 40 inches long. Both roots are about 1 inch thick. Other houses carrying gobo are Gurney, Hudson, Kitazawa, Nichols, and Redwood.

While gobo is grown mainly for the sake of its crisp, fiberless root, the young shoots are sometimes eaten also, prepared like asparagus or pickled.

The root is scraped or peeled, cut into chunks, and simmered in water until tender. Some cooks pre-scald the root before simmering. The taste is something like a pungent salsify or scorzonera.

Peeled gobo is shredded, soaked in cold water for an hour, then drained. It is then stir-fried in oil, usually peanut oil, often in combination with other vegetables such as daikon or mitsuba.

A popular combination in Japan is cooked gobo, cooked carrots, and chopped green onions, served in hot broth. Pre-cooked chicken or fish may be included.

SAUCED GOBO

2 cups gobo root peeled and cut into 1-inch pieces
1/2 cup Cathay sauce*

1 tablespoon toasted sesame seeds*

Cook gobo in boiling water until fork-tender. Drain. Add the sauce to pan and bring to a boil, remove to serving bowl, and sprinkle with sesame seeds. Makes four portions.

⌇ HAMBURG PARSLEY – Europe ⌇

This is a parsley grown for its tapering, carrot-shaped root, about 6 inches long and 2 inches wide at the top. Botanically *Petroselinum radicatum,* Hamburg parsley was enjoyed in Germany in the mid-sixteenth century, but according to early horticultural writers the Germans called it Dutch parsley. Today it is sometimes called turnip-rooted parsley.

You can use Hamburg parsley's leaves as you would ordinary parsley, but the root is the crop, and the plant needs most of its leaves to grow a good root. It will grow in partial shade, maturing in three months.

Raise Hamburg parsley as you do leaf parsley, seeding it in early spring in the garden. Dig in compost generously and spade deeply to give the root a chance to develop well. Parsley seed takes two or three weeks to sprout, so we keep it damp during that time by soaking the soil before seeding and then using the sheet plastic covering described for Chinese celery.

When roots mature, dig them as needed. They can be left in the garden where they are growing or stored for winter in a box of moist sand in the cellar.

Hamburg parsley seed is listed by several seed houses.

Hamburg parsley is a popular ingredient in soups and stews. For this purpose the roots are peeled and then sliced for the cooking.

Hamburg parsley roots can be eaten raw, thinly sliced or grated, as in a salad.

For an agreeable side dish, peel and slice Hamburg parsley roots, steam them tender, and serve them dressed with oil and vinegar.

HAMBURG PARSLEY PATE

This is an Eastern European paté or spread.

1 Hamburg parsley root
1/4 cup butter
2 cups roasted duck meat
2 green onions, white parts
  only, chopped
2 tablespoons capers

2 tablespoons chopped
  parsley
salt and pepper
2 tablespoons Madeira
commercial sour cream

Peel Hamburg parsley root, cut into cubes, put into a saucepan with the butter, cover and cook until tender. Remove from heat and put it through a grinder along with duck meat, onions, capers, and parsley. To the ground mixture add salt and pepper to taste, the Madeira, and enough sour cream to make a spreadable consistency. Makes about a pint.

CHICKEN SOUP WITH HAMBURG PARSLEY

Various versions of this soup are served in Northern Europe.

4 tablespoons butter
1 floured cut-up frying chicken
1 Hamburg parsley root, peeled
2 ribs celery including leaves,
  chopped

1 medium-sized leek cut
  in 1/2-inch slices
6 cups chicken stock
2 teaspoons salt
1/2 teaspoon pepper

Melt butter in a heavy soup pot, and sear chicken in it over medium-high heat. Reduce heat, cut Hamburg parsley into ½-inch slices, and quarter the slices. Add to the chicken, along with celery, leek, and stock. Bring to a boil, cover pot, lower heat, simmer until chicken can be removed from bones. Chop the meat coarsely and return it to soup pot. Season soup with the salt and pepper. Makes four to six portions.

Haricots are French snap beans, of which there are many excellent varieties. J. A. DEMONCHAUX CO.

HAMBURG PARSLEY SOUP

This is a Southern European soup.

1 Hamburg parsley root, peeled and shredded	2 cloves
3 onions, sliced	4 cups chicken stock
2 carrots, peeled and sliced	salt and pepper

Put all ingredients except salt and pepper in a heavy soup pot. Cover pot, bring to a boil, reduce heat, and simmer for 4 hours. Season with salt and pepper to taste. Makes four portions.

HARICOTS – Europe

Haricot is a general French word for bean, understood to mean a snap bean type, *Phaseolus vulgaris*. (Fava beans are *feves*.) Haricots are so identified with good French cooking that as far back as 300 years ago the European traveler John Josselyn referred, in *An Account of Two Voyages to New England,* to "French beans: or rather, American beans," and proceeded to describe what we now call snap beans.

The French have developed many good varieties of haricots. Triomphe de Farcy is a round-podded one, and we found it an excellent bean that would get along with less than ideal conditions. One year we grew it in a planter in a cool and often foggy climate, and it produced a reasonably good crop without complaint. This variety and others are carried by Demonchaux and le Jardin. Johnny and Thompson & Morgan each list an haricot variety, and Suttons and

Vilmorin list many.

Haricots are grown as other snap beans. Follow the directions for adzuki beans.

FRENCH BEANS

A simple and very good French way of cooking haricots is to parboil them tender but firm in salted water, drain, simmer in butter, add some cream, bring just to a simmer and serve at once. Savory is the classic herb for beans, and can be added, chopped, and sprinkled over the finished dish. Basil and parsley are good, too.

HARICOTS AND BACON

3 cups green-podded haricots	2 tablespoons butter
vegetable stock	1/2 teaspoon salt
4 strips bacon cut in 1/2-inch	1/8 teaspoon pepper
squares	1/4 teaspoon sugar

Remove tip ends of beans, snap the beans in two, put into stock in large saucepan, and cook, covered, about 40 minutes or until fork-tender. Drain, remove beans, put bacon in pan, and cook for 5 minutes. Return beans to pan, cover pan, and simmer 5 minutes. Add remaining ingredients and simmer 5 more minutes. Turn up heat, stir for a few seconds, and serve at once. Makes four portions.

HARICOTS WITH EGGS

35-40 green-podded haricots, parboiled	1/8 teaspoon freshly grated nutmeg
3 eggs	1 tablespoon herb
2 tablespoons cream	butter* (tarragon)
salt and pepper	

Line the bottom of a round, shallow baking dish with the haricots, arranging pods like the spokes of a wheel. Beat eggs lightly with the cream, season with the salt, pepper, and nutmeg. Pour carefully over the beans. Bake in a preheated 300° F. oven for about 20 minutes or until eggs are nicely firm. Melt herb butter, pour it over eggs, and serve at once. Makes two portions.

Hinn Choy's flavor is surprisingly meaty, making it an excellent vegetable for stir-frying. The leaves are the part so used. TSANG & MA INTERNATIONAL

HARICOT CASSEROLE

Casserole cooking gives a blend of flavors in this vegetable combination, which is also good served cold the next day.

2 cups yellow-podded haricots
cut into 1-inch pieces
6 courgettes cut into 1/2-inch
slices
3 green onions, chopped
2 tomatoes cut into eighths

2 garlic cloves, minced
1 tablespoon minced thyme
2 tablespoons minced parsley
1/2 teaspoon salt
1/8 teaspoon pepper
4 tablespoons butter

Combine all the ingredients except butter with gentle stirring in a bowl. Transfer them to a casserole. Cut the butter into several slivers and insert these into the vegetable mixture here and there. Cover casserole and cook at 325° F. for 1½ hours. Makes four portions.

✍ HINN CHOY – Orient ✍

Hinn Choy is another ornamental plant that is eaten. Its genus is *Amaranthus,* and several of its species are cooked, usually as leafy greens and particularly in India and China. The *gangeticus* species is most widely used. The annual, Hinn Choy, also called Amaranth and Joseph's Coat (for its colorful foliage), is one of its varieties and is carried by Tsang & Ma.

Tampala, brought from China by Burpee a generation ago, is a related form of this quite variable species. "In China," Frederick Porter Smith wrote of *A. gangeticus* in an 1871 study of useful plants in

China, "the plant is eaten as a cheap, cooling, spring vegetable by all classes."

Hinn Choy is a warm weather crop in the U.S., grown much like chard. Sow seed in late spring in ordinary garden soil, and thin plants to about 2 inches apart. They are touchy about being transplanted, and with us they also take some coaxing while small.

For the first harvests, take entire plants to give others room. Thereafter harvest leaves. Under ideal conditions, Hinn Choy should mature in less than two months, making small succession plantings at 3-week intervals practical.

We would describe Hinn Choy's flavor as full-bodied, almost as if a ham stock had been used in the cooking. A friend, Marcia Marks, who is knowledgeable about Oriental foods, says of Hinn Choy, "It's very tender. When cooked, the leaves and slender stems are buttery and almost meaty."

Its hearty flavor makes Hinn Choy an excellent vegetable for stir-frying all by itself. We find a combination of oil and butter best here. For variation, sprinkle with toasted sesame seeds* when serving.

Chopped young Hinn Choy is a nice addition to a chicken soup, stirred in during the last 10 minutes of cooking.

To make a quick Chinese-style soup, crumble 4 ounces of ground fresh pork into a heavy saucepan and cook it with frequent stirring until light brown. Stir in 1 cup of chopped Hinn Choy, squeeze a garlic clove into the pan through a press, and add 2 or 3 cups of vegetable stock or water. Bring to a boil, lower heat, and simmer for a few minutes. Season with salt and pepper.

HUSK TOMATOES — Europe, Mexico, Orient

Various species of the *Physalis* genus produce edible berries encased in a papery husk. They go by the names of husk tomatoes, strawberry tomatoes, ground cherries, poha, tomatillo, cape gooseberry, and others.

Husk tomatoes are *Physalis pruinosa;* they and tomatoes belong to the same family—not a close relationship in the plant world, but husk tomatoes take the same general culture as tomatoes. Sow seed indoors six weeks before the last spring frost. Move plants to the garden when soil is warm and the air balmy. Space plants 2 feet apart

The husk tomato is often eaten as a dessert when completely ripe, shown here topped with commercial sour cream. The bite-sized fruits come encased in papery husks in which they keep remarkably well at room temperature. THOMPSON & MORGAN

in a sunny spot. They grow a foot high, sometimes more, and staking them will improve the harvest, which arrives in about three months and amounts to about two pounds of marble-sized fruits per plant.

Seed houses listing husk tomatoes include Burgess, de Giorgi, Farmer, Field, Gurney, Nichols, Olds, and Thompson & Morgan.

An agreeable feature of the husk tomato is its good storage life. Ripe fruits will keep at cool room temperatures for weeks. Fruit colors range from orange or yellow to greenish brown and purple.

The usual way in which husk tomatoes are used is in preserves. But, as in the case of pie cherries, the taste of husk tomatoes eaten as fresh fruit has an appeal for many people. For this purpose the berries should be thoroughly ripe, when they taste slightly tart but have a sweet and tomato-like flavor. A variety listed by Thompson & Morgan under the name Golden Berry is said to be in demand in London for eating fresh as a dessert. It is also dried for use in fruit cakes in place of raisins.

Another use of husk tomatoes is in tossed salads. A good international combination is curled endive, sliced daikon, and husk tomatoes, with French dressing.*

HUSK TOMATO SAUCE FOR CHICKEN

This Mexican style sauce is ordinarily made with the Physalis *species called tomatillo, but any of the others will produce an agreeably south-of-the-border-tasting sauce.*

This Indian mustard is a type called dai gai choy by the Chinese. It forms a loose head and is a favored cooking green in the Orient. TSANG & MA INTERNATIONAL

Husk enough husk tomatoes to fill a cup measure. Cook them in just a little water until they can be mashed in the pan. Add 1 tablespoon of olive oil, a finely chopped garlic clove, and two chopped sweet peppers or one sweet one and one hot one. Simmer until peppers are soft. Season with salt.

⟿ INDIAN MUSTARDS – Orient ⟿

Like the mustard greens familiar to American gardeners, the Indian mustards are members of the cabbage group, botanically *Brassica juncea*. They are annuals. One listed by Tsang & Ma is called gai choy, a type name. It is a dwarf plant, topping off at 8 inches in 5 weeks. Leaves and stems are light green with a true but nonpungent mustard flavor. A larger variety, also listed by this house, is dai gai choy. It forms a loose head and is harvested when 10-14 inches tall. Kitazawa carries what appears to be this same variety under the name Chinese Heading mustard, and Redwood lists a South China Heading. Kitazawa lists several other Indian mustards, including the red-leaved and white-stemmed Aka Takana. Fairly pungent when eaten raw in salads, it becomes mild though not bland when cooked.

These mustards all should be grown like Chinese cabbage, and like them, the mustards are spring or fall crops. Three-inch spacing is recommended for gai choy and Aka Takana—10 inches for the others.

Indian mustards are cooked like other leafy greens: steamed quickly or stir-fried in a little oil or butter with no liquid except the water that clings to the leaves after rinsing. They mix well with other greens, and when used alone need very little seasoning.

GAI CHOY SOUP

Finely chop a cupful of gai choy leaves. Bring 4 cups of chicken stock or broth to a boil, and add the gai choy. Simmer for 5 minutes and season to taste with salt and a tablespoon of grated ginger root. (Preserved ginger is a substitute for the fresh root; half a teaspoon of it, minced, would be the right amount here.)

San Francisco's Chinatown markets sell stems of dai gai choy, with the leaves stripped off. These stems are bought for pickling and are a popular appetizer in Chinese restaurants. To pickle the stems, use any pickling recipe.

Dai gai choy stems cut into thin slices are stir-fried with thinly sliced beef. A little grated ginger can be added for seasoning during the last minute or so of cooking.

Tsang & Ma suggest this Chinese soup: Cook chopped dai gai choy stems with peeled and coarsely chopped sweet potatoes in water for about 3 hours. The result is a mildly sweet soup. About 1 cup of each vegetable and 4 cups of water are satisfactory proportions. Add water if needed during the cooking, and season soup lightly with salt.

⌐ ITALIAN BEANS – Europe ⌐

The Italian bean is also known as the Italian green pod bean. It is closely related to the familiar snap bean—both are *Phaseolus vulgaris* and annuals. The Italian pole variety called Romano is the original. A newer bush variety is listed as Bush Romano, and there is one called Roma.

Seed houses listing strains of Italian beans include Burpee (Romano and Roma), Harris (Romano and Bush Romano), Nichols (Romano and Roma), Park (Roma), Stokes (Bush Romano), and Thompson & Morgan (Romano).

The taste reference often applied to Kentucky Wonder beans is also often applied to Italian beans—a "beany" taste, which is true. The Italian is an excellent bean, and even when harvested later than it should be, its pods, in our experience, do not become fibrous. These pods are wider than those of snap beans and flatter. Average lengths are usually given as 4½ inches for bush type, 6 inches for pole ones. But we have had pods 8 inches long and of top quality. The plants are known for good production.

Culture of Italian beans is the same as for snap beans. Follow the directions for growing adzuki beans.

Like snap beans, Italian beans are ordinarily eaten pod and all, but can also be shelled out. The beans are about the size and shape of a small plump lima and are lightly buff-colored with sometimes a greenish tinge. When cooked whole, the beans are prepared by snapping off tip ends.

SAUCED ITALIAN BEANS

A good Italian way to serve Italian beans that have been cooked tender in water or vegetable stock is to accompany the drained beans with a cruet of French dressing* or one each of olive oil and red wine vinegar and a side dish of chopped chives for each diner to sprinkle over the beans in the amount that suits his taste. The beans are served warm.

ROMAN SALAD

3 cups Italian beans cut in 2-inch lengths	1 tablespoon minced basil
vegetable stock	1/4 teaspoon salt
1 garlic clove	1/8 teaspoon pepper
1/4 cup olive oil	1 hardboiled egg, chopped
1 tablespoon white wine vinegar	1 cup croutons*

Cook beans in stock until barely fork-tender. Drain. Squeeze garlic clove through press over beans. Add oil, vinegar, basil, salt, and pepper. Toss lightly. Add egg and croutons. Toss briefly again and serve. Makes four portions.

The salad can be made beforehand and chilled for use later. The croutons in this case should be added just before serving.

ITALIAN SALAD

An Italian bean salad said to have been invented by Garibaldi's cook was probably the inspiration for this one, as they differ in only a few details and procedures.

3/4 cup olive oil	2 cups sliced Italian tomatoes
1/4 cup red wine vinegar	2 green onions, chopped
2 anchovies, mashed	1/2 cup chopped basil
4 cups cooked Italian beans, chilled	salt and freshly ground pepper
2 cups sliced boiled potatoes, chilled	

Combine oil, vinegar, and anchovies, stirring well, to make the salad dressing. Spread beans in a shallow pan and pour dressing over them. Let them marinate in it for an hour with occasional lifting and turning with pancake turner.

Remove beans and put them in salad bowl with the potatoes, tomatoes, onions, and basil, mixing gently. Season to taste with the salt and pepper, and dribble the dressing over all. Tossing is not necessary. Makes eight portions.

ITALIAN PARSLEY — Europe

The curled parsley universally seen in the markets is prettier than Italian parsley, but once you taste the two, one after the other, you will see why good cooks choose the Italian, a flat-leaf kind. It consistently gets higher marks on flavor.

Botanically, parsley is *Petroselinum crispum,* and to grow it, you must have patience at first, for it is a slow germinator. But so is curled parsley. We often seed in a flat, cover the flat with sheet plastic, and in three weeks it is sprouting without further attention. When seeding directly in the garden, we proceed as described for Chinese celery. Parsley will grow without thinning, but to get the best plants, space them 6 inches apart.

Parsley will take a good deal of shade, and once started it is an undemanding plant. It is a biennial, so the plants you grow this year will present you with early parsley next spring before they shoot up flower stalks to form seed, their last act. An easy way to get young plants is to let the old ones go to seed. Some of the seed will sprout and you can then transplant the seedlings—or let them grow where they stand. Doing the new seeding yourself is a better way, though, as you can have replacement plants ready for cropping by the time the old ones go to seed.

Most seed houses list an Italian parsley, and de Giorgi lists a giant one that they say is the variety called Celery-Leaved or Neopolitan. We have grown it and can testify that it attains 3 or more feet in height in time. A dozen plants supply bushels of leaves.

When cooked with onions, parsley calms the strength of the onions and is said to prevent onion after-taste. Raw parsley eaten after garlic acts as a breath sweetener. Parsley also is known to help increase the flavor of other herbs in a dish.

PARSLEY SOUP

2 tablespoons butter	1 clove garlic
1 cup finely chopped Italian parsley	1 quart rich milk
	2 egg yolks, beaten
2 green onions, chopped	salt and pepper
1/4 cup chicken stock	grated Parmesan cheese

Melt butter in saucepan over low heat. Add parsley and onions. Simmer 2-3 minutes. Add stock and garlic clove squeezed through press. Cover pan, simmer 10 minutes.

In a separate saucepan bring milk to scalding. Remove from heat, stir a little of the milk into the egg yolks, then add egg yolks to the milk, stirring. Return pan to low heat and simmer, stirring until mixture thickens. Add contents of the other saucepan, and salt and pepper to taste. Stir to blend well, but be careful not to let soup boil. Serve with the cheese sprinkled over soup in each bowl. Makes four portions.

︶ ITALIAN TOMATOES – Europe ︶

Another name for Italian tomatoes is paste tomatoes, for these meaty little fruits with few seeds are splendid for making tomato paste. They are also very good peeled and sliced for a salad, and can be used in many dishes calling for tomatoes. Tomatoes are botanically *Lycopersicum esculentum*. They are annuals in temperate climates.

Like other tomatoes, the Italian ones need a long warm summer and are usually started indoors six to eight weeks ahead of the arrival of warm weather, when they are then set in the garden in a sunny spot where a 4-inch layer of compost has been worked in, along with a pound of cottonseed meal to 20 feet of row. Two feet between plants is sufficient spacing if the plants are staked. They are allowed

The meaty little Italian tomatoes, so liked for making tomato paste, are good in many other ways too. This one is the variety Roma VF. JOSEPH HARRIS CO.

to ramble on the soil in commercial plantings, but you'll get cleaner fruit and easier harvesting by staking them.

Deep-water tomatoes twice a week (½ bucketful per plant) or every other day in dry weather, and give them a 4-6-inch mulch of compost when half-grown and ½ cup of cottonseed meal per plant.

There are several varieties of Italian tomatoes. San Marzano is a good old one that has been supplanted to some extent by Roma. In eleven weeks both start bearing large crops of blocky little red fruits about 3 inches long. Burgess and Burpee carry both, and Roma is carried by Harris, who introduced it, and by Ledden and Olds. Stokes carries five Italian tomatoes.

Italian tomatoes are noted for bearing tremendous crops over a long season.

SKILLET TOMATOES

4 tablespoons butter	1/2 cup flour
1 garlic clove	1/2 teaspoon salt
4 cups Italian tomatoes cut	1/4 teaspoon pepper
in 1/2-inch slices	2 tablespoons minced basil

Melt butter in large skillet. Squeeze garlic clove into it through press and stir to blend. Dredge tomato slices in the flour seasoned with the salt and pepper. Put dredged tomatoes into skillet and cook until they are light brown on both sides. Serve sprinkled with the basil. Makes four portions.

This dish goes well with fried beef liver.

FRESH TOMATO SAUCE

This simple Italian sauce is for use over hot foods: pasta, or such vegetables as young globe artichokes, finnochio, Italian beans. A blender will make enough of it quickly so that the surplus can be stored in the refrigerator.

6 garlic cloves, peeled
1/4 cup olive oil
1/2 cup chopped basil
1/4 cup chopped Italian
  parsley

4 ripe Italian tomatoes,
  peeled
1/2 teaspoon salt
vegetable oil

Put garlic and half the olive oil into blender. Blend at medium speed a few seconds. Add basil and the rest of the olive oil. Blend at medium speed a few seconds. Add parsley and half the tomatoes. Blend at high speed for several seconds. Add the rest of the tomatoes and the salt. Blend at high speed for several seconds. Wipe down sides of blender jar with rubber spatula and add enough vegetable oil, or more olive oil, to bring total to the 2-cup level. Give a final blending at high speed until mixture is uniformly smooth.

MEDITERRANEAN TOMATOES AND BEANS

This delicious southern European dish is made with the meaty little Italian tomatoes.

1 cup dried white beans
6 green onions, white parts,
  chopped
1 garlic clove, minced
2 tablespoons olive oil
2 cups coarsely chopped
  Italian tomatoes

1 teaspoon minced marjoram
1 teaspoon minced thyme
1/2 cup chopped Italian
  parsley
1 teaspoon salt
1/4 teaspoon pepper
lemon rind

Soak beans overnight in about a quart of water. Next morning transfer beans to saucepan, add more water to cover if needed, and cook covered until beans are just tender.

Meanwhile put onions, garlic, and olive oil in large saucepan and cook gently 5 minutes. Add tomatoes and herbs, simmer covered 30 minutes. With a potato masher, mash the mixture right in the sauce-

pan. *Add beans, and if more liquid is needed, add vegetable stock or water. Consistency should be somewhat more liquid than that of baked beans.*

Cover pan, simmer 30 minutes longer. Add salt and pepper, and twist lemon rind over the dish just before serving. Makes six portions.

TOMATO PASTE

2 quarts Italian tomatoes   salad oil
1 tablespoon salt

Peel and chop the tomatoes. Put them into a saucepan, sprinkle them with the salt, and let stand 3-4 hours. Put pan on medium-low heat, bring to a simmer, cook until tomatoes are soft, stirring frequently. Mash to a puree in the pan with potato masher, or press tomatoes through a sieve.

Continue cooking with frequent stirring until tomatoes are reduced to a pulp dry enough to be spread in a layer-cake pan. Score the pulp in the pan several times with a knife, and put pan in a 130° F. oven to dry. Knead the pulp occasionally until it is dry enough to roll between the hands.

Keeping the paste in the cake pan, dry it at room temperature four more days. Then make marble-sized balls, roll them in the oil, and store them in a jar with waxed-paper cover at room temperature. They will keep perfectly for months. If they become too dry for easy handling, roll them again in oil.

To use them, crush a ball in a little boiling water to dissolve it, then add to the dish being flavored. One ball supplies the flavor of up to half a cup of cooked tomatoes.

QUICK TOMATO SOUP

This is a convenient way to make a fast luncheon soup for two. Drop 1 or 2 balls of tomato paste, as prepared in the previous recipe, into ½ cup of boiling water. While the balls are softening, melt two tablespoons of butter in a saucepan, stir in 2 tablespoons of flour, and simmer over low heat briefly to make a roux. Stirring, slowly add 1½ cups of milk and bring just to a simmer. Stir in tomato mixture. Remove from heat. Season with salt and pepper and a whisper of sugar. Serve at once with a pinch of minced parsley floating on top.

Kale is an attractive leafy green of the cabbage genus, not nearly as well-known in America as in Europe. Highly nutritious, kale has the merit of taking cold weather well, providing garden-fresh fare in winter. W. ATLEE BURPEE CO.

⟿ KALE – Europe ⟿

We were of two minds about including kale here, feeling that it is not really exotic. Yet, we keep encountering gardeners who have never grown it, usually have never tasted it, and in some cases have never heard of it. Despite this, kale was known by the ancient Romans and is widely appreciated in Europe, where it is particularly associated with Scotch tastes. It is also known as borecole and as colewort, and the collard is a sub-variety of kale. Kale is one of the cabbage plants, *Brassica oleracea* var. *acephala,* grown as an annual, and harvested one leaf at a time.

One of kale's great advantages is its tolerance to cold. It will brave freezes, and in the Midwest we gave it no winter protection. In fact, cold weather improves its already good flavor. It is also one of the vegetables highest in vitamins.

To grow kale, follow the directions for Chinese cabbage. Kale, however, will accept transplanting. It can also be seeded in the garden where it must stay. Pick kale leaves young, starting with the lowest.

Most seed houses carry one or more kale varieties, and Hudson lists one of the seldom seen marrow-stem kales, whose leaves develop especially thick and meaty midribs.

COLCANNON

Even though it is customarily made with cabbage and potatoes, this famous Irish dish is said to have begun as a kale and potato combination.

4 green onions, finely chopped
1/2 cup butter
3 cups finely chopped kale
3 cups mashed potatoes

1/2 cup of cream
salt and pepper
butter

Simmer onions in butter until they are soft. Cook kale in very little water until it is tender. Drain off any water. Combine onions and kale with potatoes, which should be warm. Stir well. Stir in cream, salt, and pepper. Pile mixture into baking dish, dot generously with butter, brown lightly under broiler. Makes four portions.

A German variation of colcannon, instead of stirring the kale and mashed potatoes together, puts them in a baking dish with the kale on the bottom, topped by the potatoes, which are mixed with a beaten egg. The whole is then dotted with butter and baked 15 minutes in a hot oven.

PORTUGUESE KALE SOUP

This fine, filling main-dish soup is good on a cold winter night and is popular with the Portuguese, according to a friend of Portuguese descent.

3 cups chopped kale
2-3 cups of cooked dried
 garbanzo beans
3 cups diced potatoes
2 cloves garlic, peeled

1 large onion, sliced
4 cups water
1 teaspoon salt
1/4 teaspoon pepper

Put all ingredients except salt and pepper into soup pot. Simmer 2 hours, adding more water as needed. Stir in salt and pepper and adjust seasoning if needed. Makes six to eight portions.

Beef, sausage, or fish sometimes are included in this soup. Half a pound to a pound of any would be about right.

⌇ KOHLRABI — Europe, Orient ⌇

Like kale, kohlrabi is not nearly as well known in America as abroad. Yet, among those familiar with this other cabbage-group plant, *Brassica caulorapa*, some consider it the finest flavored brassica of them

Kohlrabi is another excellent brassica not at all well-known in American gardens, though highly thought of in Europe. The edible portion is the bulb shown here, developed just above ground level. JOSEPH HARRIS CO.

all. A biennial grown as an annual, kohlrabi apparently originated in the Mediterranean region. The edible part is a bulblike swelling of the stem just above ground level. The swelling is about the size of a turnip and takes two months to mature. In the south of Europe, the more tender leaves of kohlrabi are also eaten. In our experience the leaves are too coarse to be of much use, but a variety of kohlrabi called Prague is said to have tender leaves. De Giorgi carries one—Prague Special, which is a fast grower. Old kohlrabi bulbs become woody, so harvest a little ahead of full maturity for best results.

You can seed kohlrabi directly in the garden in spring for an early summer crop and in August for an October crop. It will not flourish in hot weather, and it won't take as much cold as most of its relatives. In other respects, follow growing directions given for Chinese cabbage, except that you can transplant kohlrabi if you do so carefully, taking a good ball of earth with each plant. Careless transplanting produces woody bulbs.

Many seed houses carry a kohlrabi variety, usually the Early White Vienna or Early Purple Vienna. The first has white flesh, the other, greenish-white. Both are good.

To harvest kohlrabi, cut the stem near the base of the bulb and remove the leaves. Bulbs store fairly well for several days in the refrigerator. You can also start the harvest early and continue it daily or as needed over two weeks. Bulbs of the late crop can be stored in a cool basement in a box of moist sand after leaves and lower stem have been trimmed off.

To prepare kohlrabi for cooking, take a slice off the top of the bulb, remove any stub of stem on the base, and then peel the bulb as you would a potato.

Kohlrabi can be used raw in salads, cut in thin slices, strips, or dice.

Garden-fresh kohlrabi cooks in about 10 minutes when steamed or simmered in water or vegetable stock. It can then be served with merely a sprinkle of salt and lemon juice, or it can be dressed with a sauce. Hollandaise sauce* is excellent for this purpose.

KOHLRABI BRAISE

3 tablespoons butter
3 kohlrabi bulbs, peeled
lettuce leaves
2 eschalots, finely diced

1/4 teaspoon salt
1/8 teaspoon ground ginger
1/4 cup dry white wine

Melt butter in skillet. Slice kohlrabi into ¼-inch rounds, add to butter, and simmer for a few minutes. Turn slices, cover with lettuce leaves, put lid on skillet, and cook over low heat 10 minutes or until kohlrabi is tender. Discard lettuce, remove kohlrabi to serving bowl with slotted turner, and keep warm.

Put eschalots into butter and juice remaining in skillet. Simmer briefly over low heat. Add salt and ginger. Stir in wine. Turn up heat and cook, stirring, for a few seconds. Top kohlrabi with this sauce and serve at once. Makes four portions.

KOHLRABI ITALIENNE

4 kohlrabi bulbs, peeled
1 teaspoon anchovy paste
2 tablespoons olive oil
2 cups peeled and chopped
  Italian tomatoes

1/4 teaspoon salt
sprinkle of freshly ground
  pepper
1 clove garlic

Cut kohlrabi into ½-inch slices. Steam tender, about 10 minutes.

Meanwhile mix anchovy paste with olive oil, put into skillet, add tomatoes, and simmer 30 minutes. Season with the salt and pepper and garlic squeezed through press. Put the kohlrabi slices into the skillet and simmer a few minutes while basting slices with pan liquids. Makes four portions.

The leek has no business remaining as elusive in American home gardens as it does, for its seeds are not hard to find. Yet the leek, *Allium porrum,* a hardy biennial grown as an annual, qualifies for inclusion here, because to most American gardeners it is exotic, somewhat known but not grown, a delicacy bespeaking Continental tastes.

Aside from needing a long time to grow, the leek is not really a difficult plant. A seedsman who feels strongly about the leek's image, J.A. Demonchaux, states firmly: "Given the right amount of water and fertilizer (plenty of both), leeks will grow almost everywhere (slowly but surely)." Seeding to maturity takes about four months. You can seed in flats, for a head start, and transplant. Or seed directly in the garden in early spring.

A partly shaded site will do. A heavy feeder, the leek wants 4 inches or more of compost worked into the seed bed, and a pound of cottonseed meal to 15 feet of row. When plants are about six weeks old, thin to 6 inches apart. You can transplant thinnings or eat them. When plants are two months old, a side dressing of fertilizer and a compost mulch is helpful. Drawing the mulch close to the plants will help blanch them, but don't draw it up so high that it can sift down between leaves.

As leeks mature, some send up sprouts from the roots—little new plants. These can be pulled free when the mature mother leek is harvested, and then the little ones can be transplanted. Give them winter protection, as with a strawy mulch, and they will reward you with an early crop the following season.

You need not harvest a leek until you need it. Mature ones will take winter cold, so they can be stored right where they are growing. A straw mulch on them will make digging easier if the ground is frozen. The edible part of a leek is the thick white section at the bottom, but with a garden-fresh leek the green leaves are tender enough to be eaten also, especially the lower two-thirds. The white part of a well-grown leek can be 2 inches wide and 6 inches long. A variety called Unique can grow up to 8 inches long. Most seed houses list leeks, and Stokes has an especially good selection. Vilmorin carries nine varieties, and Suttons six, all with a wide range of seasonal adaptation.

To prepare a leek for cooking, cut off the roots with a slice of the bottom, and trim away the top third of the leaves, making a diagonal cut from each side so that the leafy top resembles an inverted letter V. The bases of the leaves take a good deal of rinsing to free them of soil that inevitably sifts down into them, so we just split the leek lengthwise to clean it.

VICHYSSOISE

4 tablespoons butter
4 leeks, thinly sliced
4 green onions, chopped
1-1/2 pounds of potatoes,
 peeled and chopped

4 cups chicken stock
2 cups of milk (half & half)
salt and pepper
finely chopped parsley

In heavy saucepan melt butter, add leeks and onions, simmer briefly. Add potatoes and half the stock. Cover pan, cook until vegetables are soft. With a potato masher, mash vegetables in the saucepan. Add remainder of stock, bring to a simmer. Stir in the milk and remove pan from heat just before soup comes to a boil. Let stand, covered, for a few minutes. Season to taste with salt and pepper, and serve at once in warm bowls, garnishing with a pinch of the parsley. Makes four portions.

Vichyssoise is even more famous as a cold soup. Simply chill and omit the parsley garnish until serving time. Stir the chilled soup well before serving.

LEEK SOUP

The leek is the national emblem of the Welsh, but it was a main food source of the Irish for centuries, along with oatmeal. The two are used in this Irish soup:

4 large leeks
1/4 cup butter
2 cups chicken or beef stock
1/4 cup old-fashioned rolled oats

2 cups milk
salt and pepper
1 teaspoon minced
 parsley

Trim off all but about 2 inches of the leek leaves. Cut leeks in half lengthwise, wash well, and chop into ½-inch pieces. Melt butter in saucepan and cook leeks in it 10 minutes. Add stock, bring to a boil, add rolled oats. Cover pan and simmer about 30 minutes with occasional stirring. Then add milk, bring to a simmer, remove from heat, and season to taste with salt and pepper. Serve with a sprinkle of parsley floating in each bowl. Makes four portions.

COCK-A-LEEKIE

Another leek soup is this Scottish dish, although it is also almost a stew. Put a cut-up stewing chicken into a soup pot, cover with water, add a dozen medium-size leeks or eight large ones that have been cut in half and rinsed, and cut into ½-inch pieces. Bring to a boil, then simmer for about 2 hours or until chicken is tender, skimming fat from time to time. About 30 minutes before the soup is done, add a handful of seeded dried prunes, and season to taste with salt and pepper.

DUTCH LEEKS

A Dutch way of fixing leeks is to cut and rinse them as in the previous two recipes, then simmer in a vegetable stock such as water in which cabbage has been briefly cooked. The leeks are then drained and served with Bechamel sauce* or a medium white sauce to which is added a teaspoon or two of vinegar or lemon juice.

LEEK SALAD

A German leek dish, served cold as a salad, is made by cooking half a dozen large leeks in water or vegetable stock until just tender, draining and chilling, then dressing with a blend of ½ cup commerical sour cream, 2 tablespoons lemon juice, 1 teaspoon or more of horseradish, salt and pepper.

MAO GWA – Orient

Mao gwa is a Chinese variation on the familiar summer squash. Also called Chinese fuzzy gourd and wax gourd, mao gwa, *Benincasa hispida,* is related to the Chinese winter melon, doan gwa. But since mao gwa, an annual, is harvested young, it takes less time—about 3 months—from seeding to table than the winter melon.

Follow growing directions for doan gwa, and harvest mao gwa when the plump, somewhat pear-shaped fruits are about 5 inches long. This applies to the Chieh-Que variety, listed by Tsang & Ma. There is also a ball-shaped variety of mao gwa, but we know of no retail source of seed for it.

Mao gwa is prized for its thick white flesh. Prepare a mao gwa for cooking by rubbing off the fuzzy coat with a paper towel, like

These plump fruits, about the size of pears, are the Chinese fuzzy gourds, mao gwa, liked for their thick white flesh. TSANG & MA INTERNATIONAL

defuzzing a peach, and then removing the skin with a potato peeler. Next, cut the fruit in half and scoop out and discard any central core. The halves can then be stuffed like summer squash and baked at 350° for about an hour. A popular combination for the stuffing is finely chopped mao gwa flesh, green onions, and ground fresh pork.

Mao gwa is also sliced into soups and can be cooked in the same ways that doan gwa is cooked.

⤳ MITSUBA – Orient ⤳

This plant is also called Japanese parsley but is not related to our parsley. Mitsuba is botanically of the *Cryptotaenia* genus; the specific name is given as *japonica,* and the plant appears to be identical to the description given by Sturtevant[1] under the species *canadensis;* but botanical names can change over the years. Mitsuba is a perennial, liking moist shady sites and a compost mulch, and growing to about 2 feet tall. It can be harvested some three months after it is sown.

Mitsuba seed sources are Kitazawa and Nichols.

The parsleylike leaves and blanched stems of mitsuba are put in salads and are also cooked as greens, alone or with other cooking greens.

Both leaves and stems are put into soups as a flavoring. Mitsuba is strongly aromatic, so some experimenting is in order to see how much of the flavor you want to add to a dish.

---

[1] E. Lewis Sturtevant, *Sturtevant's Edible Plants of the World,* ed. U.P. Hedrick (Albany, N.Y.: J.B. Lyon Company, 1919). Reprinted 1972 by Dover Publications, New York, N.Y.

For a different cooking green, and one that appears on many French tables, grow orach, *Atriplex hortensis*. It is also called mountain spinach, French spinach, sea purslane, and butter leaves. A succulent green with a somewhat spinach taste, Orach was known to the ancient Greeks and Romans and was introduced to England in Elizabethan times, when it became favored for cooking with sorrel to tame sorrel's tartness.

Orach is an attractive plant, its arrow-shaped leaves varying from pale green to light red. It can grow up to 6 feet, although it is often much shorter. A hardy annual, it should be seeded in spring or fall, and thinned 6 to 12 inches apart. It is generally a willing grower and needs only ordinary garden care.

Only the young leaves are eaten, old ones growing too fibrous. Houses listing orach are Hudson, Nichols, and Redwood.

In cooking orach, treat it like spinach or chard.

ORACH AND ALMONDS

1/4 cup olive oil
1 clove of garlic, minced
4 green onions, chopped
6 cups orach leaves coarsely
  chopped

1 tablespoon lemon juice
1/2 teaspoon salt
sprinkle of freshly ground
  pepper
1/4 cup slivered almonds

Heat the oil in large saucepan. Add garlic and onions. Cook 10 minutes with occasional stirring over low heat.

Add the orach, cover pan, cook over medium heat 5 minutes. Sprinkle with lemon juice, salt, and pepper. Stir to blend. Serve sprinkled with the almonds. Makes four portions.

ORACH AND POTATOES

This recipe from northern Europe is reminiscent of the Irish dish colcannon, given under kale.

4 cups rinsed and finely
  chopped orach leaves
4 cups freshly cooked mashed
  potatoes

4 tablespoons butter
1 teaspoon vinegar
1/2 teaspoon salt
1/4 teaspoon pepper

Stir the orach thoroughly into the potatoes, which should be warm, in a saucepan over medium-low heat. Cook for a few minutes with occasional stirring. Then add the rest of the ingredients and continue stirring until the butter is melted and all ingredients are well-blended. Serve at once. Makes four portions.

⌇ ORIENTAL CUCUMBERS – Orient ⌇

The typical Oriental cucumber is much longer than the familiar kind and is apt to be smaller in diameter, sometimes curvy, and sometimes bulbous at the blossom end. Both are *Cucumis sativus* and annuals. Some Oriental ones can grow nearly 2 feet long without tasting bitter or losing crispness. Fruits of the Soo Yu variety, for example, mature at 18-20 inches in length in our garden, average 1½ inches thick, and weigh about a pound each. As with other cucumbers, however, Oriental kinds can be eaten at younger stages of growth if wished.

A warm summer is a fairly standard requirement for growing cucumbers, but there are some Oriental ones that thrive in cool weather. One such is Early Ochai, listed by Johnny.

Many American seed houses carry one or two varieties of Oriental cucumbers (and the fairly new one called Burpless is Oriental).

To grow cucumbers, follow the directions given for Cee Gwa, and give the cucumbers deep watering, a half-bucket per plant, about three times a week or oftener when weather is dry.

Older cucumber vines produce few male flowers, so to keep getting good, well-shaped fruits—the result of good pollination—plant a few cucumber seeds near the first planting after the first vines are well-grown. If your summer is long enough, you will collect some fruit from this second planting, a kind of bonus for good husbandry.

It is important to pick cucumber fruits. If they are allowed to remain on the vine much beyond maturity, the plants will cease to produce. This is because their object in life is to continue the breed by growing seed—and once they are allowed to mature fruit, the job is done. This is true of annual plants generally, but cucumbers seem to be particularly aware of it.

In the Orient, cucumbers appear on the appetizer tray frequently. One way they are prepared is by being sliced paper-thin, then soaked in brine. Before serving, they are drained and slightly dried. A proper strength of brine for this purpose is 2 teaspoons of salt dissolved in 1 cup of water. A 30-minute soaking will suffice, and the drying can be done by pressing slices between paper towels.

Another appetizer is made by removing a core from the center of a cucumber, filling the hollow with a mixture such as grated daikon and chopped shrimp. The stuffed cucumber is cut into ½-inch rounds for serving. A fast way to hollow the cucumber is to cut it in half the long way, remove the center of each half with a spoon or a ball cutter, and then pin the halves together with toothpicks after each half is stuffed. Space toothpicks ½ inch apart and slice between them to cut the rounds.

STIR-FRIED CUCUMBERS

1 20-inch Oriental cucumber (about 1 pound)	salt and pepper
1/4 cup peanut oil	1 tablespoon minced Chinese chives
1/2 cup chicken stock	

Peel cucumber and cut into ¼-inch slices. Put slices into large heavy skillet, add oil, stir-fry until slices are nearly translucent. Add stock and continue stir-frying for about 2 minutes. Season lightly with salt and pepper and sprinkle with the Chinese chives when serving. The chives are not cooked. Makes two portions.

ORIENTAL EGGPLANTS – Orient

Just like Western eggplants, Oriental ones, which are also *Solanum melongena* and annuals, insist on lots of warm weather—about ten weeks of it. By and large, the Oriental varieties make smaller plants than eggplants we are used to, some being small enough in plant, leaf, and fruit to be considered dwarf plants. But they are not small in production. Whereas a standard eggplant will give half a dozen big fruits, it is not uncommon for an Oriental eggplant to produce forty or more.

Depending on variety, these fruits range in size from 4 to 12 inches long and from 1½ to 3 inches across at the widest point. Today, many of the varieties are hybrids.

Seed eggplants indoors in peat pots two months before warm weather. In the garden they want full sun and rich soil. We find eggplants so demanding of the maximum sunlight that it is useless to plant them in a spot affording less; and this applies as rigidly to Oriental ones we have tried as to others. Work compost generously into the planting spot beforehand, along with 1 pound of cottonseed meal to 15 feet of row. Space plants about 2 feet apart, and when they are half grown, spread a compost mulch. Deep watering is very welcome, about a half-bucket per plant twice a week, or oftener in dry weather.

Oriental eggplants are listed by Field, Hudson, Johnny, Kitazawa, le Jardin, and Nichols.

You can harvest Oriental eggplants before they mature, although we prefer to let them arrive at the mature, glossy-skin stage, which is when Western eggplants are picked. But don't let them stay on the plant too long. When you cut the eggplant to cook it, look at the seeds. They should be white and soft. Brown seeds mean the fruit is over-mature. There is no indication of this on the outside, so you have to learn to judge it by experience.

Eggplant fruits can be stored in the refrigerator for up to 10 days, but they lose quality at refrigerator temperatures. For this reason alone, the smaller size of Oriental eggplants is recommended. The harvest regulates itself conveniently for the cook.

It is our practice to peel eggplants, but this is a personal prejudice. Not everyone does peel them, including Oriental cooks. Also, we do not salt eggplant slices to drain out moisture before cooking— but many people would proceed in no other way.

An Oriental way of cooking eggplant is to cut it into slices ¼ inch thick, dip them into tempura batter*, and fry them in oil. A skillet is satisfactory here, or the slices can be cooked in deep fat.

BAKED EGGPLANT FINGERS

3 cups finger-sized pieces of eggplant
1/3 cup oil
1 Welsh onion, white part, chopped
1 cup Chinese celery cut in 1/4-inch pieces
1 clove of garlic
1/3 cup meat stock
1/4 teaspoon salt
1/8 teaspoon pepper
1 teaspoon minced mitsuba leaves

In skillet cook eggplant in the oil until light brown. Remove eggplant to baking dish. In the oil remaining in skillet cook onion 2-3 minutes. Squeeze garlic into skillet through press, add celery and stock. Cook over high heat a few minutes, stirring. Add salt, pepper, and mitsuba, pour over eggplant in baking dish, bake at 325° F. for 40 minutes. Makes four portions.

DALMATIAN EGGPLANT

This European recipe was given to us by a friend born in Transylvania. We have found that an Oriental eggplant provides a more convenient size slice for this purpose.

Peel the eggplant and slice it thinly, no more than 1/8 inch thick. Brush the slices lightly with olive oil. Sprinkle salt lightly on a heavy skillet or griddle, and fry the eggplant slices on both sides. They should be rather crisp when done and are used in the same manner as potato chips.

ORIENTAL PUMPKINS – Orient

Oriental pumpkins, although treated differently by Asian cooks than we handle our Western pumpkins, are botanically the same—*Cucurbita pepo*. They are annuals and differ only in varieties. Seed for them is scarce in this country, and we know of only one seed house, Redwood, that lists this vegetable. The variety carried is Futtsu Early Black. It matures in 4 months, or a little less, and is a small flattish fruit, 6 or 7 inches wide and 4 inches high. The skin is the dark green of an acorn squash, and the flesh is yellow.

Oriental pumpkins are grown like other cucurbits; follow the directions given for courgettes, but space the pumpkin planting spots 4 feet apart.

Oriental cooks frequently cook pumpkin flesh with moist heat, rather than baking as we usually do, and then combine the pumpkin with other vegetables such as mushrooms and snow peas.

One way to prepare the pumpkins for this is to cut balls of the flesh with a ball cutter, as you would a melon. The pumpkin balls are then poached for 5 minutes in water or a light vegetable stock. After this they are given a final steaming and combined with other vegetables in a single dish, or they may be finished by simmering along with the others.

Slices of pumpkin flesh are cut ¼ inch thick, dredged in cornstarch, and fried in peanut oil until golden brown. These may be served with a topping of toasted sesame seeds* for added flavor.

PETITS POIS – Europe

The peas we most associate with the French are tiny. Alongside the typical pea, they look much as a golf ball looks alongside a baseball.

Appropriately called petits pois, the little peas make up for their somewhat lesser production by their sweetness and delicacy. They are botanically *Pisum sativum* and annuals.

To grow petits pois, follow the directions for fava beans. You will find two bush and one pole variety of petits pois listed by le Jardin, a pole variety by Suttons, and a pole variety by Thompson & Morgan. Vilmorin lists three bush and one pole variety.

Harvest these little peas when they are young, and try to pick them no more than an hour before you shell and cook them. The French cook them quickly, about 5 minutes, in salted boiling water. For added flavor they put a few of the pea pods in the water and discard them after the peas are cooked. Some cooks, we among them, cook the peas in vegetable stock. Either way, the peas are drained after the cooking and can then be served dressed with melted butter alone, or with butter and a little of a minced herb such as chervil.

Suttons suggest cooking petits pois with cocktail onions, chopped lettuce, and tiny carrots. The little round French carrots would be nice here.

PETITS POIS SOUP

A famous use of these tiny peas is in the classic cream of pea soup.

3 cups shelled petits pois	1 teaspoon minced tarragon
2 cups chicken stock	or chervil
1 cup heavy cream	salt

Put peas into saucepan and add just enough water to barely cover them. Cover pan, bring water to a boil, reduce heat, and simmer 10 minutes or until peas are just tender.

Transfer contents of saucepan to blender, and puree peas. Or puree them with a potato masher right in the saucepan.

Add chicken stock to pureed peas in saucepan and bring to a simmer. Add cream. Heat, stirring, and remove pan from range as soon as soup simmers. Stir in tarragon or chervil, add salt to taste, and serve in warmed soup bowls. Makes four portions.

PETITS POIS AND POTATOES

6-10 potatoes, peeled	1/8 teaspoon pepper
2 cups shelled petits pois	4 tablespoons butter
vegetable stock	2 eschalots, minced
1/2 teaspoon salt	2 teaspoons fines herbes*

Using a small ball cutter, make 100 potato balls. This will take 6 to 10 potatoes. Cook potato balls in water until tender. Meanwhile in a separate saucepan cook peas in the vegetable stock until barely tender. Drain both vegetables. Put potato balls in serving bowl, top with the peas, season with the salt and pepper.

Melt butter and simmer eschalots in it 1-2 minutes. Pour over peas, sprinkle with the herbs, serve at once. Makes four portions.

Note: We save the water the potato balls are cooked in and cook the leftover potato shells in it. They can then become mashed potatoes, or can be chopped and cooked in a skillet in butter. The potato water can be used in sauces or in place of water when making breads or rolls.

RADICHETTA — Europe

Radichetta, grown as an annual, is closely related to the common endive—*Cichorium* genus—and is popular in Italy. Its most prized crop is not its leaves (although they make an agreeably bitter addition to cooked greens), but the plump, immature flower stalks. These are produced freely in the spring, about two months after seeding. They somewhat resemble asparagus, and like asparagus, new ones keep sprouting after each cutting. Asparagus chicory is another name for radichetta. Others are Italian chicory, Italian dandelion, and ciccoria Catalogna.

Seed it in early spring in compost-rich soil. It will accept partial shade. Incidentally, we find it so tempting to birds that we must protect the bed with a cover of wire netting.

Houses listing radichetta include Comstock, Nichols, and Stokes. De Giorgi carries two varieties.

RADICHETTA SALAD

Uncooked radichetta stalks mixed with upland cress or garden cress—which are all in season at the same time—make a fine green Italian salad. Use an oil and vinegar dressing (or the French dressing* in chapter three), sprinkle the salad with croutons*, and garnish with slices of hardboiled egg.

RADICHETTA FRITTATA

The succulent radichetta stalks give this Italian omelet a springlike freshness of flavor.

2 tablespoons butter	1/4 teaspoon salt
1-1/2 cups radichetta stalks	1/8 teaspoon pepper
cut in 1/4-inch pieces	1 teaspoon fines herbes*
4 eggs	1 tablespoon butter
2 tablespoons cold water	

Melt the 2 tablespoons of butter in a 10-inch omelet pan, add radichetta, cover pan, and cook for 5 minutes, shaking pan a few times during cooking. Meanwhile, beat the eggs and water until frothy, stir in salt, pepper, and herbs. Pour this mixture over the radichetta, stir briefly, cover pan, and cook over low heat until just firm on top. Turn off heat, dot top of frittata with the tablespoon of butter. Slide under broiler until butter is melted and surface of frittata is light golden. Serve at once. Makes four portions.

⟞ ROCAMBOLE – Europe ⟝

In Europe, rocambole, a member of the onion group, is esteemed for its milder-than-garlic, stronger-than-onion flavor. Yet it is hardly known in the United States. Botanically a form of *Allium sativum,* although often called *A. scorodoprasum,* it is a perennial grown as an annual. Sometimes called sand leek, serpent garlic, or Spanish garlic it appears to have come from the Near East or Southeastern Europe. It was grown in Europe in the Middle Ages.

Like garlic, rocambole grows a segmented underground bulb and is propagated by planting the segments 2 inches deep and 12 to 18 inches apart. In mild climates, plant from fall to early spring. In cold climates, plant in spring. The plants grow about 3 feet tall and do best in fertile soil and an open site.

Rocambole often grows a bonus crop of little bulbs (bulbils) in the air at the tip of the stem instead of flowers. These bulbils can also be planted, needing two seasons to grow a full-sized underground bulb. A curious feature of this bulbil-bearing stem is that it twists into a loop on its way up (thus the name serpent garlic), looking as if a flower arranger had tied a loose knot in the stem for a startling effect. Some "garlic" we grew a few years ago from a bulb supplied by a friend, who called it Italian garlic, did the same thing, revealing itself as rocambole. And garlic does not produce bulbils.

Le Jardin lists rocambole.

If you like strong flavors, try using rocambole in place of eschalots. Mainly, however, rocambole does its best job when employed as a mild garlic. The bulbils as well as the bulb segments are so used. We find bulbils especially welcome when only a little garlic flavoring is wanted. And you need not peel them for the garlic press—just drop one or two in and squeeze. The bulbil skin will remain in the press, and this also makes cleaning the press easier.

ROQUETTE — Europe

One reason for growing roquette is that it lets you take a culinary tour of history. Roquette, also called rocket, was a salad plant in ancient Rome, grown for its slightly pungent dandelionlike leaves and its stems. It was grown for the same purpose in medieval times—the English herbalist John Gerarde calling it "a good salat-herbe."

In the early nineteenth century the Turks and Greeks were said to prefer roquette to all other salad plants, but by that time the plant had fallen in popularity in Western Europe. Today it is a garden curiosity. Botanically *Eruca sativa,* roquette is an annual plant that makes a quick growth—large enough to harvest entire plants in six weeks.

It wants cool weather, which also improves its taste, and plenty of moisture. Planted in spring and fall, roquette is grown like celtuce but doesn't insist on as acid a soil.

Roquette seed is carried by Burpee, Comstock, de Giorgi, Gurney, Hudson, le Jardin, Nichols, and Redwood.

The taste of roquette is often compared to that of watercress, but we do not agree. Roquette is stronger-flavored and distinctive. Some say roquette tastes of peanuts to them.

ROQUETTE SALAD

Combine 1 cup of torn roquette leaves and chopped young stems with 4 cups of torn curled endive heart leaves. Toss with French dres-

sing* and serve with a spoonful of commercial sour cream or yogurt topping the center of each individual bowl.

ROQUETTE AND ONIONS

3 tablespoons olive oil	salt and pepper
1 large onion, sliced	1/2 cup of 1/4-inch bread
2 cups chopped roquette leaves	cubes

Heat oil in skillet, add onion, cook over low heat until onion is translucent. Turn onion slices on other sides and add roquette. Increase heat and cook, shaking skillet now and then, until roquette wilts. Reduce heat and stir gently with rubber spatula, separating onions into rings and mingling with roquette. Season with salt and pepper, remove with slotted turner to serving bowl.

Put bread cubes into skillet with remaining liquids, turn up heat and cook, stirring, until cubes have absorbed liquids in skillet and are golden brown. Strew them over roquette and onion rings, serve at once. Makes two portions.

～ SCORZONERA – Europe ～

This plant grows a root that looks like a black-skinned salsify root and is about the size of a slender parsnip. Scorzonera is in fact sometimes called black salsify or black oyster plant. But although it also tastes oysterish, like salsify, scorzonera is not related to salsify *(Tragopogon porrifolius)* but botanically is *Scorzonera hispanica*. It is a perennial but is grown as an annual, the edible root developing fully in one season.

Sow scorzonera seed in late spring, in well-spaded earth enriched with compost and with a pound of cottonseed meal worked into 20 feet of row. Thin plants to 4 inches apart. They grow about 2 feet tall and need all season to develop good-sized roots. Dig them through the fall and winter as needed, covering the bed with 6 inches of strawy mulch in cold-winter climates. Or store roots in moist sand in a cool cellar after clipping off all but about half an inch of the stems.

Among seedsmen listing scorzonera are de Giorgi, Demonchaux, Hudson, Johnny, le Jardin, and Thompson & Morgan.

Scorzonera is slightly sweet and feels slippery. To prepare the roots for cooking, scrape or thinly peel them. They darken on this exposure to air, so to keep them white, many cooks drop them into

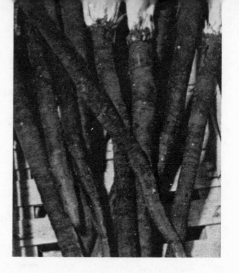

Scorzonera looks like a long slender black parsnip, but tastes agreeably of oysters. Well-regarded in Europe, it is hardly known in the United States. J. A. DEMONCHAUX CO.

vinegar water—¼ cup of vinegar to 1 quart of water. This soaking also reduces a faint bitterness. The flavor of scorzonera is delicate and can be hurt by overcooking.

SCORZONERA SOUP

1 cup grated scorzonera	1/4 cup barley
4 tablespoons butter	1/4 cup dry vermouth
1 cup chopped mushrooms	2 tablespoons minced parsley
4 green onions	1/2 teaspoon salt
4 cups chicken stock	1/4 teaspoon pepper

Simmer scorzonera briefly in the butter in a saucepan with the mushrooms and the white parts of the chopped green onions. Reserve the green onion tops. Add chicken stock and barley to the saucepan. Cover pan and simmer about 1½ hours, or until barley is tender.

Stir in the vermouth, parsley, and 2 tablespoons of the green onion tops finely chopped. Season with salt and pepper. Makes four portions.

SKILLET SCORZONERA

Allow 2 medium-sized scorzonera roots per person. Peel and cut into finger-long lengths. Parboil until almost fork-tender. Drain and cool. Dip each piece into beer batter and fry them golden-brown in sizzling butter in a skillet, shaking skillet several times. Salt lightly and serve.

BEER BATTER

Sift 1 cup flour with 1 teaspoon baking powder and ¼ teaspoon salt. Beat 1 egg lightly and stir into it 1 tablespoon salad oil and ¾ cup of beer. Gradually mix in the dry ingredients, stirring well.

SAUTÉED SCORZONERA

A simple way to cook scorzonera, and one used in Europe, is to pre-cook peeled roots chopped into 3-inch pieces in water or vegetable stock until fork-tender, 15-20 minutes. Drain scorzonera and cook in butter in a skillet until a very light golden brown. Salt and serve.

SEA-KALE – Europe

This European vegetable, sea-kale, is well worth the American gardener's attention for several reasons. It is a perennial, continuing to yield for about ten years. It supplies its own replacement plants with root cuttings. It comes to the table at a most welcome time, early spring, when there are few other things in the garden. It is both a salad plant and a vegetable for cooking.

Botanically *Crambe maritima,* sea-kale can be started with seed in flats in early spring. In six weeks move the little plants to the garden, spacing them 1½ to 2 feet apart, where they can remain in full or partial sun. Generously dig compost into each planting spot beforehand, along with 1 cup of cottonseed meal per spot.

Let the plants grow without harvesting for the first and second years. You can then start the annual harvest the third spring. This is the same timing given asparagus. A good way to go about harvesting sea-kale is to cover the plant with a box for several days. This blanches the young shoots just sprouting and makes them tender. Cut or snap them off at ground level when they are about a foot tall or less. The harvesting continues for several weeks, until the plants start leafing out.

Sea-kale grows to about 3 feet tall. In the late fall, cut the plants down to a few inches above ground level—again, the same handling given asparagus—and give them a 4-inch mulch of compost.

Thompson & Morgan list sea-kale.

For a simple and delicious dish, cut sea-kale sprouts into 3-inch lengths, steam them tender, and serve them on toast dressed with hollandaise sauce.*

BAKED SEA-KALE

2 cups of 1-inch pieces	salt and pepper
of sea-kale	1/4 cup crumbled Roquefort
1/4 cup butter	cheese

Steam sea-kale fork-tender or cook it in vegetable stock. Place sea-kale pieces in buttered baking dish. Melt the butter and pour it over sea-kale in baking dish. Season lightly with salt and pepper. Sprinkle the cheese evenly over top of sea-kale. Bake at 400° F. until the cheese is bubbling. Serve at once. Makes four portions.

SEA-KALE WITH WINE

2 cups of 1-inch pieces of sea-kale	1 cup sliced mushrooms
1/4 cup water	1/4 teaspoon salt
1/4 cup butter	1/8 teaspoon pepper
	2 tablespoons Madeira

Put sea-kale and water in saucepan, cover pan, simmer until sea-kale is fork-tender. Add butter and mushrooms, turn up heat and cook, stirring 2-3 minutes. Transfer vegetables to serving dish with slotted turner.

Add the salt and pepper to the juices in the saucepan and cook over high heat for 1 minute, tilting pan from side to side as you do so. Remove from heat, stir in the Madeira, pour over vegetables, and serve at once. Makes four portions.

SESAME — Near East, Orient

This interesting plant, botanically *Sesamum orientale* and once commonly called bene, benne, and benny, is the source of the sesame seeds used in cooking. Sesame is a native of the Asian and African tropics, so it must be grown in more northern latitudes as a tender annual, started indoors two months before the onset of mild weather, and set out in the garden in rich soil at the time tomatoes are set out. It is usually helpful to work in some wood ashes.

Sesame plants grow to about 2 feet tall and have attractive pink-and-white flowers somewhat like foxglove. The seeds are enclosed in angular pods or capsules. Harvest the pods when they ripen, and open them over a pan to catch the numerous seeds.

Sesame seed is carried by de Giorgi, Hudson, and Redwood.

Sesame seed is a popular flavoring for foods in the Orient. A recipe for the preparation of toasted sesame seed is given in chapter three.

SESAME COOKIES

A friend famous for her cookies gave us this recipe, which we found makes a delicate and delicious little tea cooky.

1 teaspoon butter
1/2 cup sesame seeds
3/4 cup butter
1-1/2 cups brown sugar
  firmly packed

2 eggs
1-1/2 cups sifted flour
1/2 teaspoon baking powder
1/4 teaspoon salt
1 teaspoon rum flavoring

Melt the teaspoon of butter in a heavy skillet over low heat. Add sesame seeds and stir constantly until golden brown.

Cream the ¾ cup of butter and the brown sugar until smooth. Beat in eggs. Sift flour again, with baking powder and salt, into creamed mixture. Mix until well-blended. Stir in rum flavoring and the sesame seeds.

Drop dough by teaspoonfuls onto cooky sheets that have been buttered and floured. Bake 15 minutes at 325° F.

SESAME BREAD RIBBONS

These ribbonlike versions of the popular bread sticks are a delicious accompaniment to spaghetti and chile con carne and are equally good for picnics and for serving with a drink.

4 tablespoons butter
2/3 cup lukewarm water
1 package yeast
1 tablespoon sugar
1 teaspoon salt

2 cups flour
1 egg white beaten briefly
  with 1 teaspoon cold
  water
2 tablespoons sesame seeds

Melt butter and set it aside to cool. Put water in mixing bowl, stir in yeast and sugar, let rest a few minutes. Then stir in, in this order, the salt, ½ cup of the flour, melted butter, another ½ cup flour. Beat batter 100 strokes. Gradually stir and knead in the rest of the flour. Dough will be soft, like roll dough. Let rise, covered in bowl, until doubled—about an hour.

Transfer dough to floured board, divide in half, roll each half into a 10-inch by 12-inch oblong. Brush surface of each with egg-white mixture. Sprinkle sesame seeds evenly over each oblong. With sharp knife cut each into ribbons ¾ inch wide and 10 inches long. You should get about 30 ribbons. Place them on buttered cooky sheets, bake about 12 minutes at 425° F., turning them upside down the last 5 minutes.

HOBIE'S SESAME SAUCE

From another friend, this one of Japanese descent, we obtained this recipe for a sauce that is used with various vegetables. It goes nicely, for example, with snow peas and with gobo.

1/4 cup sesame seeds   **about 1 teaspoon sugar**
2 tablespoons soy sauce

Put sesame seeds in a small skillet, cover, cook over medium-low heat, shaking skillet, until seeds are lightly browned.

Transfer seeds to a mortar and crush them lightly. This is done to increase the flavor. Mix in the soy sauce, then the sugar. The original recipe called for up to 2 tablespoons of sugar. We thought this too sweet, but you may want to experiment with different amounts to suit your own taste.

SHUNGIKU – Orient

This plant is a flower whose leaves are good to eat. Called shungiku, sometimes shungiki, by the Japanese, it is also known as crown daisy and garland chrysanthemum. Botanically it is *Chrysanthemum coronarium.* Another Japanese name for it, fragrant greens, suggests the flavor of the bright green leaves—chrysanthemum-like.

Shungiku is a hardy annual, grown from seed sown early in the spring. Succession plantings every two weeks can be made, for the plants are harvested very young—when only 4 to 6 inches tall—and are pulled up or cut at ground level.

Prepare a fine seed bed for shungiku, in full or partial sunlight, and seed 15 or 20 seeds per foot. No thinning is needed.

If you see something called chop suey greens in a seed catalog, it will be shungiku. Park lists it as such. Johnny and Kitazawa carry shungiku, and Hudson and Redwood each carry two varieties, a large-leaved and small-leaved.

Just for garden interest, allow a few shungiku plants to mature. In two months they will be 2 to 3 feet tall and bear attractive light yellow blossoms.

Shungiku leaves are combined in a stir-fry dish with cooking greens such as gai lohn. Peanut oil or sesame oil are usually flavored. The addition of chopped bamboo shoots adds textural interest.

Greens cooked in the Western manner combine shungiku with curled endive or fetticus. The combination contrasts a blander green with the rather decided flavor of shungiku.

SHUNGIKU SOUP

This is a Japanese recipe for a soup that is simple to prepare but has character.

1/4 cup finely chopped shungiku   2 cups chicken stock
  leaves   1-2 teaspoons soy sauce
1 teaspoon grated ginger root

Stir shungiku and ginger root together in small bowl. Heat chicken stock. When it simmers, stir in contents of bowl, bring back to simmer, and cook covered, 4-5 minutes. Flavor with the soy sauce to taste. Makes two portions.

⌣⌐ SICILIAN FENNEL – Europe ⌣⌐

A close relative of finnochio and grown the same way, Sicilian fennel is raised for its tender fleshy young stems. Another common name for the plant is carosella, and botanically it is *Foeniculum vulgare* var. *piperitum.* Sturtevant refers to it as, "The famous *carosella,* so extensively used in Naples, scarcely known in any other place," and states, "The plant is used while in the state of running to bloom; the stems, fresh and tender, are broken and served raw, still enclosed in the expanded leaf stalks."

Sicilian fennel can be seeded early in spring for an early summer crop and again in late summer for a fall harvest.

Two seed sources are de Giorgi and Hudson.

The raw stalks are eaten like celery in Italy and included in salads. The flavor is quite similar to finnochio, recalling tarragon or chervil. In fact, Sicilian fennel can be used in place of finnochio, as in the recipes we give for finnochio.

SICILIAN FENNEL WITH OLIVES

This Italian dish requires no salt, for the olives provide it. Good with broiled chicken.

2 cups chopped Sicilian fennel	1/4 cup slivered black
2 tablespoons olive oil	Italian olives
1/4 cup chicken stock	1/2 cup heavy cream

Cook fennel in saucepan with olive oil over medium-low heat for 3 minutes, stirring to coat fennel with the oil. Cover skillet and cook for another 10 minutes.

Add stock and cook covered another 10 minutes.

Stir in olives, add cream, and bring just to a simmer. Serve at once. Makes four portions.

⌒⌒ SNOW PEAS – Europe, Orient ⌒⌒

The delicious snow pea is yet to be discovered by most American gardeners. It is also called sugar pea and edible-podded pea, for its pods are tender, like those of snap beans. Botanically, snow peas are *Pisum sativum,* as are the familiar English peas. To grow snow peas, follow the directions given for asparagus peas and provide a trellis for the vines to climb.

The varieties most widely listed in seed catalogs are Mammoth Melting Sugar, a wrinkled-seed type that for us grows a seven-foot vine, although it is said to top off at 5 feet, and Dwarf Gray Sugar, an old European sort that vines to 5 feet for us, sometimes more. Mammoth Melting Sugar bears larger pods of slightly higher quality than Dwarf Gray Sugar, but it is not as productive. We have not yet grown a recent introduction, Oregon Sugar Pod, but have very good reports on its productivity and quality.

It is quite important to harvest snow peas young, as soon as the peas in the pods show up as slight swellings on the sides of the pods. This requires daily or twice daily harvesting during the month or more of bearing.

Like snap beans, snow peas are prepared for cooking by removing the tip ends. They can be cooked whole or cut up.

It takes about 10 minutes to steam or simmer garden-fresh snow

The tender snow pea is eaten pod and all and is a delicacy from the Far East that is also popular in Europe. It is just beginning to be known to some Americans. TSANG & MA INTERNATIONAL

peas tender. Stir-frying over high heat takes only 2 or 3 minutes, for the peas are cut into small pieces and cook quickly. Not as many peas can be cooked at once in this way, however.

SNOW PEAS AND EGGS

This late breakfast or luncheon dish is suggested by Tsang & Ma.

1-1/2 cups slivered snow peas	1/2 cup crab meat
2 tablespoons butter	6 eggs
2 tablespoons minced onion	1/4 teaspoon salt

Put peas and butter in skillet and cook over high heat with constant stirring 1-2 minutes. Add minced onion and continue stir-frying another minute. Add crab meat and stir-fry another minute. Add eggs, reduce heat to medium, cover skillet, and cook about 2 minutes. Remove cover, add salt, increase heat, and stir-fry for half a minute or until eggs are almost firm. Serve at once. Makes four portions.

Snow peas are very good in a beef stew. A Chinese technique worth remembering is to avoid overcooking them here. Give them a separate 3-minute parboiling or steaming, then add to the stew during its last minute of cooking before it is served.

In Japan, raw or blanched snow peas are dipped in tempura batter* and deep-fried.

SNOW PEAS VINAIGRETTE

This is a European way of using the snow pea. The same procedure can be followed with many other vegetables, such as asparagus, cardoon, haricots, Belgian endive, and cee gwa.

4 cups cooked whole sugar peas   2 hardboiled egg yolks
1 recipe vinaigrette sauce*

Put peas in shallow glass baking dish, pour sauce over peas, let marinate for 30 minutes or more in the refrigerator. To serve, transfer to bowl, put yolks through sieve, and scatter over top of peas. Makes four portions.

By adding strips of thinly cut ham or chicken breast, this dish becomes a luncheon entree.

SNOW PEAS AND DUXELLES

This is a fast and easy yet sophisticated little dish.

2 cups snow peas   1/2 cup duxelles*
2 tablespoons salad oil   salt

Cut snow peas on the diagonal into ½-inch pieces. Put them in skillet and stir-fry them in the oil for 3 minutes. Add duxelles, stir-fry another minute. Salt lightly and serve. Makes two portions.

⌒ SORREL – Europe, Orient ⌒

Sorrel is a plant whose leaves are used raw in salads and are also cooked. It is popular in Europe and very seldom seen in American gardens, for the leaves are too sharp in taste for some, although opinions differ. Some sorrel fanciers say the leaves serve as the vinegar in a salad. Dock is another name for sorrel. It is sometimes classed as a weed since it is persistent and perennial. A planting will thrive in the garden for up to five years, after which it should be dug and the roots divided for replanting, much as rhubarb is, for the benefit of the crop.

To start a planting, sow seed in early spring, spacing plants 8-12 inches apart when they are a few inches high. Sorrel takes no special

Sorrel was liked in salads for its tart vinegary leaves during King Henry VIII's time in England and is one of the perennial garden residents. J. A. DEMONCHAUX CO.

care and prefers partial shade, which helps it to grow larger and better flavored leaves. It is a fast starter and will give you its first picking of leaves when plants are a mere 6 inches high. For a long harvest season, keep flower stems cut off as they appear.

Sorrel is of the *Rumex* genus, and there are several species for which you can get seeds. If you'd like to dine on the kind Henry VIII of England had available, it is the *acetosa* species, offered in a variety called Belleville. Le Jardin and Demonchaux list it. The *crispus* species is listed by Redwood. It has curled leaves that make good cooking greens, and if you allow a few stems to flower and set seed, the stalks are attractive in dried arrangements. Both Redwood and Hudson list *patientia* species, also known as the herb patience and as monk's rhubarb. It grows to 6 feet high, about twice as tall as the others, and the young basal leaves are what is harvested.

The *scutatus* species came to England from the Orient at the end of the sixteenth century and has been a special favorite in gardens under the names French sorrel and garden sorrel. Hudson and Redwood list it. Vilmorin lists Belleville and Blonde de Lyon; the French word for sorrel is oseille.

BRAISED SORREL

This, as the sugar suggests, is a northern European way of cooking sorrel.

1/4 cup butter	8 cups washed, chopped
2 tablespoons brown or white	sorrel leaves
sugar	1/4 teaspoon salt

Melt *butter in a deep skillet, stir in sugar, add sorrel and salt. Turn heat high, stirring, for about a minute. Lower heat, cover skillet, cook until sorrel is tender. Makes four portions.*

You may wish to tone down sorrel's acidity by substituting a milder cooking green for half of it.

SORREL SOUP 1

Also favored in northern Europe is this sorrel soup.

1 cup rinsed and chopped sorrel leaves	2 cups water
2 cups milk	
2 tablespoons butter	1/2 teaspoon salt

Put sorrel in saucepan, cover, cook over low heat 5 minutes. Add butter, cook 2-3 more minutes. Add water and cook 10 minutes. Add milk, bring just to a simmer, season with the salt, and serve. Makes four portions.

This soup is sometimes thickened with a flour-and-water mixture at the time the milk is put in. For more nutrition and flavor, a meat stock can be used instead of the water.

SORREL SOUP 2

This good sorrel soup has an Italian touch.

3-pound stewing chicken, cut up	2 tablespoons minced marjoram
2 carrots, diced	1 teaspoon minced rosemary
3 celery ribs, chopped	1/2 cup shredded sorrel
1 medium-sized onion, chopped	salt and pepper
1/2 cup chopped parsley	2 tablespoons grated Romano cheese

Put into soup pot the chicken, carrots, celery, and onion. Add water to cover, put lid on pot and simmer until chicken is tender, adding more water as needed. After the first hour of cooking add parsley, marjoram, and rosemary. Remove chicken pieces, cut meat off bones, discard bones. Cut meat into slivers and return it to soup pot along with the sorrel. Bring soup to a simmer, season with salt and pepper to taste. Just before serving, stir in the cheese. Makes four to six portions.

SORREL SOUP 3

This is an eastern European version of sorrel soup.

2 cups vegetable stock
2 cups finely chopped sorrel
1 cup mashed potatoes
2 cups chicken or beef stock
1 green onion, chopped

2 tablespoons flour blended
  with 4 tablespoons butter
1/2 teaspoon sugar
salt and pepper

Put vegetable stock and sorrel in soup pot, cook 10 minutes. Stir in mashed potatoes, meat stock, and onion. Simmer another 10 minutes. Stir in flour-and-butter mixture, ½ teaspoon at a time. Simmer 10 more minutes, add sugar, salt, and pepper to taste. Makes four portions.

⌇ SPARACHETTI —Europe ⌇

Sparachetti is a kind of broccoli that does not form large sprouts. It goes by several names: broccoli raab, broccoli-headed turnip, Italian turnip, rapine, and rapone. It is a subspecies of *Brassica oleracea italica* (broccoli).

There is a spring sparachetti and a fall one. The spring kind is seeded early in spring, matures in about seventy days, and must be used quickly, as it cannot abide warm weather, and soon bolts. The harvest consists of profuse bright green, inch-wide flower buds and tender, turniplike strap leaves. Both have a broccoli flavor. Plants are fairly low, averaging 20 inches.

The fall sparachetti is like the spring one except that it is winter-hardy. Consequently it is seeded in late fall for an early spring harvest, a very convenient arrangement.

To grow sparachetti, follow directions given for its Oriental relative, gai lohn.

Seed houses listing sparachetti under one or more of its common names are Comstock (spring and fall types), de Giorgi (spring and fall), Leddens (spring and fall), and Stokes (spring).

Sparachetti is usually cooked, although the leaves can be eaten raw as part of a spring salad.

SPARACHETTI MEDITERRANEAN

2 tablespoons olive oil
2 cups sparachetti sprouts

1 cup sliced mushrooms
1/4 cup slivered salted almonds

Heat olive oil in skillet, add sparachetti, cover skillet, and cook over low heat with occasional shaking until the sparachetti is fork-tender. Add mushrooms, cook for 3-4 minutes over brisk heat, stirring. Serve topped with the almonds. No other seasoning is required. Makes four portions.

SPARACHETTI GREENS

4 cups rinsed and coarsely chopped sparachetti leaves

1/4 teaspoon salt

1 clove garlic

1 tablespoon red wine vinegar

Cook sparachetti leaves in a saucepan over medium-low heat for 5 minutes, shaking pan several times during the cooking. No other liquid than the water remaining on the rinsed leaves is needed. Season with the salt, the garlic squeezed through a press, and the vinegar. Makes four portions.

SPARACHETTI BRAISE

4 tablespoons olive oil

2 cups sparachetti sprouts

1 cup sparachetti leaves

1/4 teaspoon salt

2 tablespoons lemon juice

2 tablespoons Madeira

1 clove garlic

Heat 2 tablespoons of the olive oil in skillet. Spread sparachetti sprouts evenly over skillet bottom. Lay sparachetti leaves over the sprouts. Cover skillet and cook over medium heat until the sprouts are fork-tender. Sprinkle with the salt, stirring, and remove sprouts and leaves with slotted turner to warm serving plate.

To juices in skillet add the rest of the oil, the lemon juice, Madeira, and the garlic squeezed through a press. Bring quickly to a simmer, stirring. Pour over the sparachetti and serve at once. Makes four portions.

～ UPLAND CRESS – Europe ～

Here again is a good food plant, upland cress, that is also something of a weed. Such a plant is almost always easy to grow (grows like a weed, as the saying goes), and is also inclined to escape the garden and grow where you may not want it. So there is a plus and a minus.

Upland cress is also called winter cress for the good reason that it can grow in cold weather. Seeded in late summer, it will supply pleasantly tart leaves for salads by early December. To start it, simply sprinkle seeds on loosened raked soil, gently rake them in, tamp soil firm, and water or let the rain do so.

There are two species of upland cress. *Barbarea vulgaris* is the one usually found; it is a perennial. The other, *B. verna,* is a biennial that sometimes behaves as a perennial. Hudson lists both. De Giorgi and Redwood list what appears to be *B. vulgaris.* Although *B. verna* sprouts a little earlier, there is no significant difference to the gardener. In each case the plants grow up to two feet tall, and the cropping season ends in the spring when the flowers appear.

The principal use for upland cress is as a welcome addition to a winter salad.

The flavor of frozen snap beans can be picked up by adding a handful of chopped upland cress. Stir the cress into the beans during the last 10 seconds of cooking.

Upland cress is also used in a cress soup. For a delicious version of it, use the recipe given for Vichyssoise in the section on leeks, and stir in a cup of chopped upland cress during the last minute of cooking.

⌇⌐ WELSH ONIONS – Europe, Orient ⌐⌇

Perhaps because the "Welsh" in its name is confusing, seedsmen frequently list this onion under some other name, often adding "bunching" to it to indicate a non-bulbing character. In Japan, Welsh onions are called Japanese bunching onions.

The onions that are usually called spring onions, green onions, or scallions are smaller than Welsh onions, however. When visitors to our garden first catch sight of one of the clumps of Welsh onions spotted here and there, they invariably stop and stare. The strong tubular leaves jut about 2 feet into the air after the first year and provide a fine gray-green accent in a bed. Fertile soil encourages such growth.

Botanically *Allium fistulosum,* this onion came originally from Siberia, arriving during the seventeenth century in Europe, where it looked so different that it was dubbed with the German name for foreign, "walsch," now called Welsh and probably mistakenly capitalized since it has nothing to do with Wales. It has been suggested, though

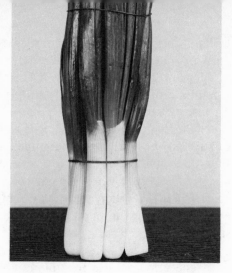

Full-grown Welsh onions rival some leeks in size, but Welsh onions are perennial, and the entire green tops are edible. W. ATLEE BURPEE CO.

not widely, that the Welsh onion may be the ancestor of all onions.

A perennial grown from seed, the Welsh onion increases by dividing its stalks during the growing season, so that each becomes several, while at the same time producing a flower head that sets about a teaspoonful of seed or more. The plant self-seeds readily, a convenient way to get a little new family of Welsh onions (which you can scoop up and move if you want them elsewhere). There is another Welsh onion type that does not divide its stalk, but we know of no American seedsman who lists it.

We give our Welsh onions a fertile seed bed to start with, and thereafter a light dressing of compost mulch repeated two or three times a year suffices. Plants seeded in spring will provide medium-sized stalks in about 4 months.

We have seen it recommended that only the leaves of Welsh onions be harvested. They are like giant chives. We do this while the plants are going through their flowering, stalk-multiplying phase. But at other times we harvest either leaves or entire stalks, whichever we wish at the time. To harvest the whole stalk, select an outside one and pull it gently away from its fellows.

Welsh onions are listed by Burpee (as Evergreen Long White Bunching), Demonchaux, de Giorgi (as Prosperity), Hudson, le Jardin, Kitizawa, Redwood (an early type and a late one), and Thompson & Morgan.

Welsh onions, leaf and stalk, are strong enough to be interesting and mild enough to be eaten raw, especially the leaves in a salad.

SAVORY WELSH ONIONS

white stalks of 4 Welsh onions   1/2 cup fine dry bread crumbs
1/2 cup French dressing*   1/4 cup butter

Cut onions into 2-inch lengths and marinate 30 minutes in the dressing. Drain. Roll onions in bread crumbs. Heat butter in skillet, put onions gently in, and sauté over medium heat about 15 minutes with occasional lifting and turning to cook them on all sides. Makes four portions.

ONION-TOMATO CASSEROLE

6 tablespoons butter   2 tablespoons red wine
12 Italian tomatoes cut in halves   vinegar
1 cup green tops of Welsh onions 1/4 teaspoon salt
   finely chopped   1/8 teaspoon pepper

Melt butter in skillet. Place tomatoes in it, cut sides down, cover, simmer 5 minutes. Remove half the tomatoes with slotted turner and place them, cut sides up, in a casserole large enough to accommodate them snugly. Spread onion tops over them and cover onion tops with the rest of the tomatoes, cut sides down. Add the vinegar, salt, and pepper to juices in skillet, cook rapidly, stirring, 1-2 minutes. Pour over vegetables in casserole, cover casserole, bake 20 minutes at 400° F. Makes four portions.

WELSH ONIONS AND SAUSAGE

This is a western European dish. Use pork sausages with medium-hot seasoning, preferably the skinless links.

1 pound pork sausages   1/2 cup cider
2 large Welsh onions, chopped   dried rosemary (optional)

Put sausages in large skillet, fry over medium heat 5 minutes, turning to brown evenly. Stir in onions, cover, cook 5 minutes more. Add cider, increase heat, cook with stirring until cider is reduced to half. A pinch of rosemary can be added during the last minute of cooking. Makes four portions.

In the Orient, Welsh onions (or Japanese bunching onions) are used in these ways:

Thin slices of the raw onions are dropped into bowls of soup as a garnish, just before serving.

Grilled steak rolls are flavored by rolling thin pieces of steak around short lengths of split onions, using the white parts, then grilling on a hibachi.

Short lengths of the white parts of onions are dipped in tempura batter* and deep-fried.

SOURCES OF SEEDS FOR THE PLANTS COVERED IN THIS BOOK

Burgess Seed and Plant Company, P.O. Box 3000, Galesburg, MI 49053. A well-established house in the upper Midwest that handles a number of unusual plants among its listings.

W. Atlee Burpee Company, Warminster, PA 18974; Clinton, IA 52732; Riverside, CA 92502. Dating back to 1876, this large and progressive seed house with an extensive breeding and trial program, has an international trade. It carries several plants discussed in this book, expands its listing of exotics from time to time, and has a helpful customer-service department.

Comstock, Ferre & Company, 263 Main Street, Wethersfield, CT 06109. This house traces its beginnings to a small operation begun in 1820. It has been in business under its present name since 1853, and its selective listing includes several exotic vegetables and a good assortment of herbs.

De Giorgi Company, Council Bluffs, IA 51501. The interesting and informative catalog includes some vegetables found nowhere else, and there is some accent on Italian specialties. Catalog 35¢.

J. A. Demonchaux Company, 225 Jackson, Topeka, KS 66603. This fairly new Midwestern house imports a selection of interesting seeds from France, a convenience to gardeners not caring to cope with translations and exchange rates.

Farmer Seed and Nursery Company, Faribault, MN 55021. Short-season varieties are a specialty here, and this reliable old house carries a number of unusual vegetables.

Henry Field Seed & Nursery Company, Shenandoah, IA 51602. Several hard-to-find vegetables are among the good selection in this house's helpful catalog.

Grace's Gardens, Autumn Lane, Hackettstown, NJ 07840. The small colorful catalog of this recently established company features some Chinese vegetables and unusual varieties, often outsized ones, of a score or more of others. Catalog 25¢.

Gurney Seed & Nursery Company, Yankton, SD 57078. The large-page catalog is made for browsing, with exotics and curiosities tucked here and there throughout. Gurney's is another of the old seed companies.

Joseph Harris Company, Moreton Farms, Rochester, NY 14624. An excellent and dependable house that conducts an extensive breeding program. The no-frills catalog is instructive and carries some uncommon vegetables.

J. L. Hudson, Seedsman, P.O. Box 1058, Redwood City, CA 94064. This small house, formerly in Michigan, carries an immense number of plants, including a good many covered in this book. Hudson issues two catalogs, a free small one listing vegetable seeds, and a larger one that includes some vegetables and is compiled alphabetically by botanical names. The latter costs 50¢ and merits the title of handbook.

Johnny's Selected Seeds, Albion, ME 04910. This New England house carries seeds of many foreign vegetables, has plans to list more, and emphasizes the production of adapted varieties by organic methods. The neat catalog includes many vegetables covered in this book. There is a charge of 50¢ for it.

Kitazawa Seed Company, 356 W. Taylor Street, San Jose, CA 95110. The listing is small, but the Oriental vegetables carried include some not obtainable elsewhere.

Orol Ledden & Sons, Sewell, NJ 08080. This well-established, medium-sized house includes several unusual vegetables despite a listing smaller than those of some seedsmen.

Le Jardin du Gourmet, West Danville, VT 05873. Foreign, particularly French, seeds are the specialty of this small house. At one time, le Jardin was almost the only U.S. mail order source of eschalots for the home gardener, and these remain one of their leading items. The herb list is good here also.

Metro Myster Farms, Route 1, Box 285, Northampton, PA 18067. Although only a few vegetable seeds are listed, they include some exotics.

Nichols Garden Nursery, 1190 N. Pacific Highway, Albany, OR 97321. The catalog, another one made for browsing, includes many unusual foreign vegetables and more herbs than are carried by any other seedsman we know of. Catalog 25¢.

L. L. Olds Seed Company, 2901 Packers Avenue, Madison, WI 53701. The explicit catalog descriptions of this long-time seed house in the upper Midwest are helpful, and the listings include a number of interesting vegetables and some rarities.

Geo. W. Park Seed Company, Greenwood, SC 29647. This southern house has a long-standing name for quality and for a broad choice of listings in its well-illustrated catalog. Herbs are one of the specialties.

The Redwood City Seed Company, P.O. Box 361, Redwood City, CA 94064. This young house issues a small catalog well worth attention for the large number of exotic plants it lists. Both common and botanical names are used, and the conversational descriptions are interesting and intelligent. Catalog 25¢.

Stokes Seeds, Box 548, Buffalo, NY 14240. This well-established northern house with Canadian connections has a good selection of unusual plants. Descriptions are frank and informative, and the plump catalog offers a wide choice.

Suttons Seeds, Reading, England. The added expense and trouble of ordering seed from abroad is somewhat offset by the interesting experience of dealing with a foreign seedsman. Suttons is an old English house whose quiet-looking little catalog brims and bubbles with gardening chat and advice. Keep American growing conditions in mind when reading descriptions. (An American house—Bryant & Cook, P.O. Box 488, South Windsor, CT 06074—carries a small selection of Suttons seeds; if they have what you want from Suttons, ordering is gratefully simple.)

Thompson & Morgan, 401 Kennedy Boulevard, Somerdale, NJ 08083. This is another long-established English seed house, and since it set up a U.S. branch office a few years ago, ordering is no problem. Prices are in U.S. money, the handling charge is nominal, and payment by personal check is practical. The colorful catalog is sprightly, the tone British-American, and the listings include several unusuals.

Tsang & Ma International, 1556 Laurel Street, San Carlos, CA 94070. This young house carries a small but interesting group of Chinese vegetables, more than half of which have been almost impossible to find in the U.S. until now. It plans to expand its listings.

Vilmorin-Andrieux, 4, Quai de la Megisserie, 75001, Paris, France. If you read French, this businesslike, attractive catalog should be little or no trouble. If you don't read French, a French-English dictionary teamed with personal gardening know-how will do the job—slowly but triumphantly. Placing an order poses the eternal international-currency problem, but the reward is an international gardening experience. And Vilmorin's listing sparkles with many an exotic. (Le Jardin and Demonchaux carry a good many of them, by-passing the ordering problem.)